Successful Women
Think *Differently*

Valorie Burton

HARVEST HOUSE PUBLISHERS
EUGENE, OREGON

Published in association with the literary agency of Alive Communications, Inc., 7680 Goddard Street, Ste #200, Colorado Springs, CO 80920.

SUCCESSFUL WOMEN THINK DIFFERENTLY
Copyright © 2012 by Valorie Burton
Published by Harvest House Publishers
Eugene, Oregon 97402
www.harvesthousepublishers.com

Library of Congress Cataloging-in-Publication Data
    Burton, Valorie, 1973-
    Successful women think differently / Valorie Burton.
       p. cm.
    ISBN 978-0-7369-3856-3 (pbk)
    ISBN 978-0-7369-4268-3 (eBook)
    1. Christian women—Religious life. 2. Success—Religious aspects—Christianity. 3. Thought and thinking—Religious aspects—Christianity. I. Title.
    BV4527.B88 2012
    248.8'43—dc23

                                2011022640

Printed in the United States of America

13 14 15 16 17 18 19 20 / VP-SK / 10 9 8

Acknowledgments

I am so grateful for the opportunity to do the work that I am called to—inspiring women to live more fulfilling lives. It is my divine assignment in life, one that I could not do alone. I want to acknowledge those who have helped get this book into your hands.

To the dedicated team at Harvest House, thank you so much for your enthusiasm and belief in me and my work—especially LaRae Weikert, Bob Hawkins, Jr., and Kathleen Kerr.

To my family, especially Johnny Burton, Jr., Leone Adger Murray, and Wade Murray. I am so blessed to have your love and never-ending support. I love you with all my heart. An extra thanks to you, Mom, for fostering my love of books and writing before I was even old enough to go to school. My writing career did not begin with my first book, but with our bedtime stories and letters to Grandmama and Grandaddy.

To my assistant, Erika Davis, for keeping me on track. Thank you for your dedication, organization, and positive attitude.

To Andrea Heinecke, Oscar Turner, and Gregory A. Campbell, thank you for your belief in me and stretching me to go to new levels with my work. I appreciate you.

To God, for inspiring my passion for helping people be resilient, happy, and purposeful. Thank You for yet another opportunity to inspire women to live fully.

Table of Contents

Introduction

---*---

IT'S ALL IN YOUR MIND

If you have ever watched other women—no more talented than you—excel beyond your level of success or happiness, then you've likely wondered what made the difference. What makes one woman succeed at high levels while another—with seemingly more resources and experience—falls short of similar goals? Consider Michelle and Angela. The two women had known each other since grade school. They were like two peas in a pod, right down to their love of all things creative—fashion, music, art, and dance. They decorated each other's bedrooms with the creativity and passion of young Martha Stewarts. They grew up in the same neighborhood, had many of the same teachers, and shared similar home environments.

Yet glimpses of which one would be more successful could be seen even in their childhood. Michelle was the better student, but she was afraid to fail. She made safe choices to ensure she'd always succeed. She was a people pleaser, so she chose a career path that would please her parents and impress her peers: law. But Michelle wasn't passionate about law. She longed to do something outside the box, but fear paralyzed her from ever taking a step forward.

Underneath the studious façade was a creative mind who loved interior design. That was her passion, but could it pay the bills? With so much time, energy, and money invested in law school and her career, she felt trapped and unwilling to pursue the dreams and desires of her heart. And anyway, the money was great. Even though she wanted to spend more time with her husband and five-year-old twin girls, she knew it was unreasonable to expect too much—great money *and* a flexible schedule. Truth be told, things looked picture-perfect from the outside, but inwardly Michelle was unfulfilled by her work, frustrated in her marriage, and disgusted by her growing waistline. She had little time for exercise and even less for the people who mattered most. Her work wasn't meaningful in a way that she longed for.

It had been almost ten years since she'd talked to Angela when she saw her at their high school reunion. As they caught up on each other's lives, Michelle sensed that Angela was genuinely happy. Unlike Michelle, Angela had pursued her dreams directly. Her philosophy was, "If it doesn't work out, I'll try something else. But why not go for what I really want first?"

Her philosophy paid off. Angela was in charge of model home interior design for a national homebuilder with real estate projects around the country. It was her dream job and she worked mostly from home, which was terrific since her daughter was not yet old enough for school. The road to success had been rocky. At each step along her path, there had been moments where fear crept in and threatened to steal her resolve. But each time, she had mustered the courage to push through. She was passionate about the work, which made it easier to persevere. She expected bumps in the road, and was not deterred by them. Instead, she was intentional about learning from them. And when she had no idea how to move forward in her marriage or career, she was intentional about seeking out information, learning to be a better communicator, and becoming more patient. Angela's life was by no means perfect, but it was successful. It had meaning, it was fulfilling, and she felt like she was living on purpose.

Angela was not more talented or smarter than Michelle. The key to Angela's success, as this book will show, is that successful women *think* differently. They make decisions differently. They set goals differently. They bounce back from failure and adversity differently. They tap into their innate strengths differently. Fortunately, their habits are teachable. Consider this book a short course—a coaching program designed to help you learn them.

My guess is that you already have some measure of success. After all, the kind of woman who picks up a book on success is typically already successful to some degree. But you know, deep down, that you've only scratched the surface of what's possible for you. You may often be praised for your accomplishments thus far, and yet you sense there is something more for you to do and be. Maybe you already know what the big goal is, but for some reason it feels elusive. I believe our paths have crossed because your full potential does not have to remain elusive. The purpose of this book is to give you that edge—a boost that gets you moving to the next level in your personal and professional life. It is a level that brings you not just accomplishment, but greater happiness.

Sometimes you may find yourself feeling stuck as you desire to move forward. Perhaps you've had some setbacks and wonder if your dreams will ever come together. Maybe you haven't even articulated what you *really* want: to do so would be to admit there is something you want that you might not get. It's easier to pretend you never wanted it than to go after it and fail. The disappointment would be too great. The embarrassment too, well, embarrassing. Or maybe, just maybe, you feel guilty about your desire for higher levels of success. After all, you're a woman. Society sometimes sends messages that leave you feeling guilty about looking for success beyond family—the implication being that such success means you are somehow neglecting your family or personal life. It is a pressure men generally do not experience to the same degree. In fact, a recent study showed that women feel significantly more guilt and distress about work intrusions at home—a finding that researchers speculate could be partially attributed to gender roles.* The cell phone calls and e-mails outside of work hours take a greater emotional toll on us.

After more than a decade of coaching women in almost every state in America and multiple foreign countries, and studying the massive research that exists on the subject of happiness and success, I have seen firsthand that women who succeed at manifesting the

---

* Paul Glavin, Scott Schieman, and Sarah Reid. "Boundary-Spanning Work Demands and Their Consequences for Guilt and Psychological Distress." *Journal of Health and Social Behavior,* March 2011, 43-57.

desires of their heart have a few things in common. Likewise, I have also observed some commonalities between women who struggle to achieve and sustain authentic success and happiness. Can you relate to any of these?

Successful Women	Unsuccessful Women
Courage in the face of fear	Feel sorry for themselves when things don't go as planned
A belief in their ability to navigate obstacles when they come	Give up once they fail
Relationships that strengthen them rather than weaken them	Relationships that drain their time and energy
Goals that are authentic to their deepest needs and desires	Define success by society's standards rather than their own
A sense of purpose and vision	Put successful women on a pedestal, as though there is some secret success formula they don't have access to
A perspective on life that accepts failure and mistakes as a normal part of the journey	Strive as though success is a destination, a place where she "arrives"
A habit of saying "no" to good opportunities in favor of purposeful ones	Focus on what they don't have rather than what they do have
A willingness to take risks	Are eternal procrastinators who won't get started because they fear failure and imperfection

Through the pages of this book, you will develop nine specific habits that have been proven to make you happier, healthier, and more resilient. These habits are skills that can be learned—and as you learn them, I encourage you to spread them. These are life skills every girl (and boy, for that matter) should learn in school while growing up. So as you begin to see a change in yourself, don't keep it to yourself! Share it. Pass it on. Pay it forward. Successful women are generous. They are givers who believe not only in themselves, but in the potential of others. And as they succeed, they bring others along with them.

DEFINING SUCCESS

Whatever you assume I meant by the word "successful" in the book's title is what I am guessing you want more of in your life. That word motivated you. And that's good. Most people want success, whether they define it as having a happy family or climbing the corporate ladder or building a healthy bank account or fitting into a size six dress. But before I begin sharing concepts and strategies for success, let's make sure we agree on what success is.

As I define it, success is a harmony of purpose, resilience, and joy. When these three elements flow together you will experience true success. Think of it this way: *Success is living your life's purpose and embracing resilience and joy as you do.*

Let's break this definition down further.

Purpose: Service fulfills the successful woman

Purpose is about making a difference in the lives of others. In other words, you cannot live your life's purpose unless you are in some way serving others. Although our purpose often brings us joy, it is not about us. It is always about using your strengths in the service of others. Your purpose in life answers a simple question: How is someone's life better because she has crossed your path?

Coach You:
Who do you impact?

Your Maker endowed you with gifts, talents, passions, and experiences that are unique to you. If I could travel back in time and observe you at four years old or fourteen years old, I would see traces of your uniqueness. Your strengths have been with you all along, and now it's time for you to use them. There is a greater impact for you to make, and now is the time to make it.

In 1999, I had an epiphany about my life's purpose while standing in a bookstore: to inspire women to live fulfilling lives, and to do so through my writing and speaking. At the time I was running my own public relations firm, using my gifts and talents as a communicator, but I wasn't passionate about the work. My passion was lacking because those gifts were not being used for the purpose for which I was created: to serve women.

Maybe you can relate. You've got half the purpose formula right. You're using your gifts and talents, just not in a way that ignites your passion in service to others. Or maybe you're in the right place, serving those you are most passionate about, but you lack the opportunity to maximize the use of your gifts and talents in the way you've always dreamed. It can be quite frustrating. And as we will learn in a few chapters, negative emotion generated by feelings like frustration can sabotage your ability to be successful. Living your purpose is not only what you're here for, but it also empowers you to succeed.

Resilience: Hope sustains the successful woman

As you set out in pursuit of your dreams, you will inevitably face challenges, trials, and stumbling blocks along the way. A key to your success will be developing a critical skill that every truly successful woman possesses in abundance: resilience. Nothing is perhaps more important to actually achieving success than the ability to be resilient in the face of challenges. Whatever your vision for the future, the likelihood of obstacles on the path to that vision is almost certain.

Coach You:
What is your most meaningful goal?

This is where successful women excel. They think differently in the face of fear, failure, setbacks, and challenges. They say different things to themselves in the face of such obstacles. As you read, you will learn to become more self-aware about the thoughts that knock on the doorstep of your mind. You will learn to choose which ones to let in and entertain.

Joy: Happiness empowers the successful woman

Joy empowers you to succeed. As Nehemiah 8:10 reminds us, "The joy of the LORD is your strength." Wherever you are on your life's journey, if you find a way to embrace it and enjoy it, you will already have found some measure of success.

Joy is not just about what happens in life—the little boosts of positive emotion that come when something makes you happy for a moment. Yes, that bite of chocolate will make you happy for a moment, so hey, savor it. But deeper joy comes from peace and love and knowing you are living the life you were meant to live. You can have all the little joy moments your heart can stand, but if you have to drag yourself out of bed in

Coach You:
What brings you joy?

the morning to go to a job you dislike and come home to a contentious household every evening, you are not going to feel successful. Every truly successful woman seeks peace in her decisions, love in her relationships, and purpose in her life.

One constant among all of the women you'll read about in the pages to come: They are happy with where they are in life. Though they have aspirations for the future and new frontiers they've yet to conquer, they are genuinely satisfied with how they have spent their lives so far—mistakes, triumphs, and all. As your coach through these pages, that's what I want for you too: a sense of satisfaction and contentment with your life.

Women have a unique set of concerns and challenges to navigate on our path to success. We have unique societal expectations, ones that often tell us who we *should* be. But who we *want* to be may not fit into that box. I don't know what life is calling you to, but I know that if it's your purpose, you are uniquely equipped to fulfill that calling.

Success will quite likely look different for you than it does for the woman next door or even your mother or your sister. While we are all wired a bit differently, there are some basic foundations for happiness and success that must be present. When it comes to educating yourself on what it will take for you to achieve your next level of success—living your purpose while embracing resilience and joy—you will benefit from a perspective that honors your uniqueness as a woman.

THE APPROACH

As we get ready to delve further into this guidebook, let me take a moment to tell you a little more about my approach to this topic. First of all, I don't claim to know how successful women think differently because I'm the world's most successful woman. That would be too narrow and a bit presumptuous on my part! What I have found, through my interviews and coaching experiences over the years, as well as through graduate study in the field of psychology and study of the Bible, is that there are several basic, foundational truths about women's success and happiness. So here's the practical approach you'll find in this book:

- Real-life stories of real women, just like you, who have found that harmony of purpose, resilience, and joy that defines success. You'll learn from their failures and triumphs, and most importantly, their thought processes along the journey.

- Practical, relevant research, some of it surprising, about how successful women think and approach life differently from the average woman. This research will equip and educate you with the tools and knowledge that can get you to your goals.

- Coaching questions to help you determine your next step. Successful women know that when you ask the right questions, you get the right answers. Through the book, you will find questions to help you gain clarity about who you are, where you're going, and how to get there.

- Spiritual insights to strengthen you for the journey. God made no mistakes when He created you. You were uniquely designed for success in your purpose. When you align your life with your strengths—those innate qualities you were gifted with—you will tap into a level of grace that empowers you to achieve things you could never accomplish in your strength alone. Throughout the book, you will be reminded of the power at work in you when you open yourself to His divine love and guidance.

Throughout the book, I will reference practical research from the pioneering academic field of positive psychology. Positive psychology doesn't focus on people's problems. Instead, it's the study of happiness, success, resilience, courage, strengths—all the things that empower you to thrive in life and work.

A NOTE ABOUT COACHING

As you read, you'll see that I use the term "coaching" and provide you with coaching questions. Coaching is the process of asking thought-provoking questions and providing a safe space to explore the answers, empowering you to take action, learn, grow, and ultimately get moving toward your destination.

This is where transformation takes place. While the stories and research insights will inspire you and give you practical knowledge that you can apply to your everyday life, the coaching questions will give you clarity about which steps to take next. Do not skip over the questions. Refuse to hurry through this process. Instead, savor it. If you do, I guarantee that you will experience real change before you finish this book.

As your coach through these pages, my goal is to be a catalyst. I'm just a vessel here to get a message to you. What you do with that message is up to you. I believe the power lies within you to make changes and adjustments in your life that will lead you straight to your dreams. One step at a time, one day at a time, expand and explore your options. Take action. Notice what works and what doesn't, then make adjustments. Take another step. That's coaching.

My ultimate goal is to help you develop the habit of coaching yourself. You won't always have another person there to coach you—or even a book to spark guidance and direction—but you will always have you. If you develop the skills to coach yourself, you will have a consistent advantage in life. Because your choices, the ones you make from here on out, will make the difference.

Valorie

Seven Key Decisions

———✳———

Choices that will change your life

Before we dive into the first chapter, let's stop here to establish the guiding principles for this book. They are seven personal decisions that I encourage you to embrace as a way of life. Without adopting these principles as your own, you may find the lessons in this book difficult to apply to your life.

These seven choices are a set of personal decisions for women who are serious about maximizing their personal and professional lives—women, like you, who don't want to look back ten years or twenty years from now with regret. Every woman who experiences authentic success—a harmony of purpose, resilience, and joy in her life—has incorporated these decisions into her life. As you turn these pages, you will see them at play. I am asking you right now to commit to them. They are simple but profound choices about your thought processes. No matter what you encounter on your journey towards your vision, these seven decisions will steer you in the right direction, restore peace and confidence, and boost your happiness even in the midst of challenges.

Decision #1: I do not downsize my dreams.

Perhaps Mark Twain said it best: "It isn't the things we did that we most regret; it's the things we didn't do." To succeed at a high level, you must start expecting more. Even when you don't get everything you expect, you'll get a whole lot more than if you were expecting nothing at all. The moment you choose to settle, you guarantee you'll never achieve your real dream. Choose faith over fear.

Decision #2: I focus on solutions, not problems.

The bigger you dream, the more opportunity for obstacles, challenges, and problems. Choose a mindset that sees these problems as opportunities for growth, and you will eventually walk into your vision. Just as importantly, when you focus on solutions you attract opportunities. People are so used to complainers, excuse-makers, and problem-generators that your refreshing bent toward solutions will be a success magnet.

Decision #3: I choose to be authentic.

Be yourself. Who else can you be? It takes less effort and energy to be yourself, but it also takes courage. Fear that you will not be accepted or approved just as you are can lead you to send your "representative" out into the world. She looks like the real you, but she's not. She's a counterfeit and whatever success she has is built on false pretenses that you must keep up in order to maintain success. Aim to be the best *you* possible—nothing more, nothing less.

Decision #4: I choose courage over fear.

Like problems, fear is inevitable. But it's not a stop sign. Fear is the most common obstacle to achieving true success and happiness. Fear tempts you to shrink from your authentic desires. It causes you to rationalize yourself out of a great idea. It leads you to pretend you don't really want what you *really* want. Like problems, fear is inevitable. But it's not a stop sign. Refuse to succumb to it.

Decision #5: I choose relationships wisely and nurture them intentionally.

Success doesn't occur in a vacuum. You need people, and people need you. Those with a strong support system have the resources that open doors of opportunity and empower them to manage any challenge. By the same token, there is a deep sense of well-being that occurs when we give to others, offering support, kindness, and love. Don't go it alone. Happiness and energy come in relationship with others.

Decision #6: I will actively seek feedback and use it to grow.

You need people around you who tell you the truth. Resilient women know this. And even when they don't like what they hear, they listen, process it, and ask themselves, "Is there a grain of truth to this feedback, even if it's negative?" Your limited perspective is not enough. Be humble, and use failures and mistakes as learning tools. Put yourself around people who know more than you, and learn all you can from them.

Decision #7: I know my purpose and take
daily action in the direction of my vision.

Consistency is key. If you continually take steps in the right direction, you will eventually arrive at your destination. Consistent action yields consistent results. "For a dream comes through much activity, and a fool's voice is known by his many words," King Solomon promised in the book of Ecclesiastes (5:3 NKJV).

Take a look at these Seven Key Decisions again. Are you willing to adopt them as your own? Which one stands out as your favorite? Which one will require a shift in attitude for you? Make a commitment to these seven decisions by making an agreement with yourself. Sign it as a symbol of your pledge. Post these commitments where you will see them often.

Seven Key Decisions	
Decision #1:	I do not downsize my dream.
Decision #2:	I focus on solutions, not problems.
Decision #3:	I choose to be authentic.
Decision #4:	I choose courage over fear.
Decision #5:	I choose relationships wisely and nurture them intentionally.
Decision #6:	I actively seek feedback and use it to grow.
Decision #7:	I know my purpose and take daily action in the direction of my vision.
Name:	
Date:	

Believe You Can Do It

———— ✳ ————

How you explain your success and failure predicts
more about your potential than you think

Key Lessons

- Optimism is a key to reaching high levels of success
- Adopt a "growth mindset" rather than a fixed one
- Take notice of your thoughts—and adjust them as needed

Cecily struggled with her weight for several years before her doctor gave her a serious wake-up call: she was prediabetic. She needed to lose 40 pounds and maintain a regimen of exercise and a healthier diet. The mid-afternoon vending machine runs for Little Debbies and potato chips would need to stop. So would the couch potato habits and all the excuses for why she didn't have time to exercise. But every time Cecily talked about doing better, her thoughts and subsequent words looked something like this:

I've tried before and failed. What's the point of trying again if the same thing is going to happen? It's a waste of time. I just need to accept that I'm a big woman. My mother is big. My sister gained weight after 30. Why should I think I can be any different? Healthy food is bland. I don't want it. And I'm embarrassed to work out in public. I don't want people staring at my flabby, overweight body. I can't do this.

With these thoughts, Cecily set out to do what the doctor suggested.

As you can imagine, her efforts were short-lived. Her counterproductive thoughts overpowered her intentions. Actions follow thoughts, and counterproductive thoughts will always send you in the opposite direction of your goal.

Think back for a moment to a recent failure. Maybe it was a relationship that went south or a promotion you were denied or a decision that got you into hot water. Or maybe it is something simpler—a test you failed or that 21-day diet that you'd already given up on by day two. Got a failure in mind? We all have them. Now, answer this question honestly and without too much thought: Why did you fail? Jot down the first things that come to mind. Just a short bullet-pointed list:

Did you write down your reasons? If not, don't skip that part. Write it down.

It's a simple exercise, but noticing how you think about failure can tell you a great deal about how high you will ascend on the success ladder. Numerous books will tell you that to be successful, you should simply emulate successful people. It can be tempting, then, to observe a woman who has achieved success, whether in her relationships or finances or health or work, and take notes about the steps she took to get to her destination. Why is it, then, that you can take two women with very similar backgrounds, education, and experience, and one excels while the other languishes? Why does one clear the hurdle when she faces it and the other trips and falls flat on her face, never to get up again? Why does one set big, compelling goals while the other settles for far less than she seems capable of?

Many of the answers to these questions cannot be found by simply observing the steps each woman chose to take. The more important insight is to understand what caused one of them to take those steps—to even *think* to take those steps—while the other did not. The edge the successful woman has over the average is in her thought processes. It is not external, but internal. Sometimes it is learned through experiences and parental examples. However, some aspects of the thought process come very naturally to you. You are either more optimistic or pessimistic in your thinking. Although you may naturally lean in one direction or the other in the face of a challenge or opportunity, an optimistic thinking style can be learned.

Let me be specific about what I mean by these two terms. The hallmark of a pessimist is that she tends to believe negative events in life will last forever, will impact everything she does, and are all her fault. But when faced with similar circumstances, the optimist believes just the opposite. She sees the event as a temporary setback, believes it is limited to this specific instance, and doesn't blame it all on herself. Instead, the optimist sees all of the external circumstances that contributed—other people, poor timing, and even God's will.

So let's go back to that recent failure you identified a moment ago and take a look at the reasons you gave for it. Re-read what you wrote. Then, answer one more question: Are all of your reasons personal faults and character traits? In other words, are your reasons things that you can't do anything about or are some of your reasons changeable?

Women who are most successful explain their failures in terms of things they can take control over. In other words, they realize they have weaknesses and faults, but those are not the sole reasons why things go wrong. Instead, they focus on the external reasons—people who made things more difficult, the fact that they weren't as prepared as they could have been, the fact that the economy was bad, the weather was bad, the boss was having a bad day again.

None of these reasons have permanent implications. After all, next time she can prepare better, the weather may improve, the economy won't be bad forever, and even if the boss keeps his job, she can always find another boss to work for in another department or company.

Failing this time doesn't mean failing next time. With a few intentional tweaks and changes, the next go-round will be a clean slate.

The successful woman is hopeful. She is empowered by knowledge of lessons gleaned from the failure of the previous try. She doesn't take failure personally and she knows that failing doesn't make her a failure. She knows that internalizing failure is a death sentence for her dreams. After all, if you're a failure, what's the point of attempting to be a success?

This last question is critical. The two thinking styles—optimistic and pessimistic—produce specific results. Numerous studies illustrate that pessimists don't persevere. They give up more easily. They become depressed more often. And for women, this is even more pronounced. We are twice as likely as men to experience depression, and the average age of the first onset of depression is now just 14 years old—half the age it was just a few decades ago.* Because we experience higher highs and lower lows emotionally than men do, we can be more sensitive to the emotional impact of our goals and efforts to reach them. Having an optimistic thinking style results in feelings that encourage us to persevere in the face of challenges.

Consider the girl who sets out to sell Girl Scout cookies. Her goal is to sell 20 boxes in front of the grocery store on Saturday. When her four-hour shift is over, she has sold just four boxes. You ask her what happened and the conversation goes something like this:

> **You:** I'm sure you were disappointed. Why do you think you only sold four boxes?
>
> **Girl:** I'm no good at selling anything. My mom said she had a sales job once and she's no good at it either. Nobody likes these cookies that much. I hate bothering people. Everybody's on a budget these days and all the women say they're trying to lose weight and can't eat sweets. I don't know if I'm going to bother going back next Saturday.

---

* Mayo Clinic, National Institute of Mental Health.

Now, I know you're not a little girl, but sometimes when it comes to self-talk that little girl voice emerges and it can sabotage your success. The eternal pessimist explains her failures as personal (flaws or traits that have no hope of changing), permanent (the problem will exist forever), and pervasive (the personal flaw that caused the failure will sabotage your success in other ways too). Psychologists call it your "explanatory" or thinking style. I call it the determining factor in whether or not you will be as successful as you are capable of being. The sooner you start paying attention to what you say to yourself about your life, your circumstances, and yes, your failures, the sooner you will break through to the next level.

LEARNING TO FAIL FORWARD

At 28, Meredith Moore became the youngest director in the McDonald's Corporation. But her stellar career didn't start off so stellar. A series of bumps could have bruised her, but instead took her on an inner journey that landed her in a role reporting to the president of one of the most recognizable brands in the world.

When Meredith graduated from Howard University with a degree in communications, the Minnesota native took a job at an international financial services firm. Initially she was trained to be a stockbroker, but passing the licensing exam proved to be struggle. Still, on the job she was a star performer her first year—an accolade she thought would be rewarded. But in the stodgy "good ole boy" environment, her talent wasn't as great an asset as she'd imagined. "The HR rep at the company said something peculiar after my first year and I've always remembered it: 'Talented people push back.'" In other words, talented people see where there is room for improvement and expect that others want to improve. Talented people question the status quo. Talented people are driven to succeed and therefore they notice what's happening—or not happening—that might impede success. The culture was not a good fit and Meredith was soon reassigned from the East Coast to the Midwest.

"The company was stuck in 1955," she reflects. "They didn't want new people." If the culture had been the only problem, she may have been able to persist longer, but soon Meredith found that her competence was being called into question on a regular basis—something she'd never experienced before. For years, Meredith had confidence in her ability to write—it was something that brought her a sense of joy and accomplishment. It was a gift she'd honed over the years, especially in college. Now, she had a supervisor who told her plain and simple, "You can't write." To make matters worse, the supervisor refused to offer any feedback on what exactly she needed to improve. "I had always been pretty good at assessing my abilities. Since childhood, I had been a good writer. The organization beat me down so much that I started to say to myself, 'I'm not a good writer.' But my job in marketing and communications was 90 percent writing."

Work was becoming a struggle as Meredith attempted to please a boss who couldn't be pleased. "It was a toxic environment. I tried every chain of contacting the human resources department, mentors, or anyone I thought could help me improve the situation. Everyone said, 'Just hold on.' Eventually, though, they said, 'We can't help you.'" Meredith felt isolated in more ways than one—in a company with few prospects for advancement, in a town she had no connection to, many miles from family or the friends she'd had in college, and with no church or community connections. She knew she needed to come up with a game plan. Although her parents advised her to stick it out, that advice felt unbearable to Meredith.

"I had never quit before," Meredith says. "But the pivotal moment for me was when I began to doubt myself. That had never been my mode of operation." It was Meredith's self-sabotaging thoughts that concerned her more than anything else. She understood something at a young age, a critical key to success for women: successful women *believe* in themselves. They have an authentic confidence that buoys them in the face of challenges and opportunities. Without that confidence, Meredith would lack the fuel to reach her goals. So she quit, and she did so quite unconventionally. One night, fed up, she decided never to go back to work at the company she'd called her employer for a year and eight months. "I packed up in the middle of the night, cleaned up my apartment, took my cat, and drove to Chicago. I left with no job."

Meredith immediately landed a job that was essentially an internship with an ad agency. At $10 an hour, it was a far cry from her very comfortable paycheck plus benefits at the financial services firm. She was adamant though, that she had made the right decision. "I learned my worth and value. I was only making $10 an hour, but I wasn't being disrespected. I was willing to let go of all of my earthly belongings to avoid having people treat me badly," she says. No one understood her decision to leave, especially her parents. But Meredith learned a key lesson through the experience. Previously, she said, she always felt she needed other people to validate her pain and her experiences. But something clicked for her the night she decided to pack up and leave. "I figured out that if I experienced it, it was valid. Other people don't need to validate my pain in order for it to be real."

Her leap of faith wasn't without a net for long. For one, she had her sister and a new church home where she felt inspired and grounded. Then opportunity knocked. "I had forgotten that I applied for a job at McDonald's Corporation while I was still at the previous company," she remembers. The company, headquartered in a suburb of Chicago, called a week and a half into her internship with the ad agency and offered her a job as a communications supervisor. She would be supporting the Chief Operating Officer of McDonald's USA with research for the financial writing needs of the company.

"There are times when you just know that God has a hand in your life," she says. "There is no way I could have ordained that." Still, she admits, "It felt like a setback because I wasn't getting the chance to write." But she was in the right place at the right time, and the doubts about her writing abilities had dissipated since leaving.

She struck up a conversation with the COO one day. He asked her, "What do you see as your next step here?" It was just the question Meredith wanted to hear. "I think I can be one of the writers," she answered. He took notice of her answer—clear and concise, and simple enough for him to act on. "He let me start helping out on some of his stuff. For example, he had an upcoming trip to Pittsburgh and let me look at his speech. I gave him some feedback." And he did the one thing she'd hoped for at her last job: he offered *her* feedback. "I loved that he would tell me why something did or didn't work! I needed that. I could learn!" Within six months, the COO promoted her to communications manager. And when he was promoted to president of the company, the communications demands of his office increased, along with Meredith's responsibilities. She became external relations manager, and then director of external relations and brand outreach, making her the youngest director at the multi-billion-dollar McDonald's USA.

LESSONS FOR FAILING FORWARD

Meredith didn't specifically set out to become the youngest director in the company. She aimed to find a place where her talents could be appreciated, where she could learn and grow, and where a mentor would be an advocate for her. When asked what's next, she mirrors the same approach that has worked for her so far. "I don't know what my goal is. I've had such accidental blessings, but I've been ready for them when they showed up," she says.

I see it a bit differently. Meredith is the type of woman who aims for passion and excellence. It is a strength so innate to her approach to life that she doesn't even call it a goal, but it leads her to succeed at high levels. She is prepared when opportunity knocks. "I don't know what my experiences are preparing me for, but I'm excited about it," Meredith says. "I'm optimistic about my future. My thirties are looking pretty good!"

We can see many of the seven decisions in Meredith's story. She refused to downsize her dream, chose courage over fear, actively sought feedback, and focused on solutions instead of problems. Here are a few more lessons:

- She refused to internalize the negativity she experienced at her first job. Instead, she attributed her failure there to the culture of the company and the stubbornness of her boss rather than exclusively attributing the problems to her own character flaws or lack of ability.

- She failed forward. She was willing to take a step back in order to find a better path.

- She took a risk.

- She took decisive action by cutting her losses and starting over.

- She believed in herself.

- She knew herself, and was able to decipher between "her stuff" and "other people's stuff." When others' negative issues tried to redefine who she was, she recognized it as "their stuff" and didn't make those issues her own.

- She volunteered to help with assignments outside of her job description so that she could demonstrate her abilities and also learn and grow.

- Sometimes sticking it out is not the best option. Sometimes you need to push the reset button and start again.

In Meredith's case, a pivotal shift occurred when she realized she was beginning to be pessimistic about her abilities and doubt herself in a way she never had before. She was self-aware, and she knew her new thoughts were a threat to her future success. She innately understood that she had to turn those thoughts around. She knew it would be an uphill climb to change her thoughts in such a toxic environment, so she changed environments.

We'll talk a bit more about self-awareness later, but for now, just keep in mind that succeeding at the next level will mean becoming much more aware of your thoughts. What are you telling yourself about your failures? Is it "I always mess up" or "I was exhausted today"? Is it "Nobody will spend money on my products in a bad economy" or "I've got to find the people who are still spending money despite a bad economy"? If your mind were an electronic billboard for the world to see, what are the thoughts they'd get to read? It takes intention to accurately capture your thoughts. With practice, you can notice them and approve the ones that help you, inviting them in and repeating them as often as needed to move you to the right actions. It's all about your thinking style in the face of failures or disappointments.

WHAT'S YOUR MINDSET?

Dr. Carol Dweck, a professor of psychology at Stanford University, has spent much of her career studying the mental attitudes of the most successful people—young and old—in the face of challenges and opportunities. What she has discovered is a fundamental difference in the *mindset* of the most successful people.*

Her quest began early in her career as she engaged in research to better understand how people cope with failure. She observed young students grappling with problems, using puzzles as the method of problem solving. Beginning with fairly simple puzzles, she then had students move on to harder ones. Her goal was not to see who finished the puzzles fastest or had the easiest time solving the puzzles. Instead, she studied each student's thought process by observing the strategies they used to solve the problem and probing their thoughts and feelings during problem solving.

She noticed that a handful of students in her studies did something peculiar compared to the others: they welcomed challenge. They were excited by the puzzles they had trouble solving. The harder the puzzle, the more determined they seemed. While other students were motivated by the possibility of looking smart and were deflated by feelings of discouragement in the face of the difficult puzzles, these students were not intimidated. When these "peculiar" students appeared to be failing because they couldn't solve the puzzle, they didn't even seem to view the experience as failing. Instead, they clearly thought they were *learning*.

What Dr. Dweck pinpointed through her research can profoundly impact how you approach your entire life—from career and relationships to health and financial habits. She called this simple but fundamental difference "fixed mindset" and "growth mindset."

A fixed mindset is focused on talent. Someone with a fixed mindset

* Carol S. Dweck, *Mindset* (New York: Ballantine Books, 2006).

believes statements like "You are smart and therefore you will do well in life" and "You are naturally gifted and that will take you far." Those who have a fixed mindset believe that one's natural gifts and abilities determine how far one can go in life. These are the people who believe that one's intelligence is defined by one's IQ, GPA, and SAT scores. These numbers become not just a measure of potential, but a limitation of potential. Those blessed with very high scores in a particular area of life gain a sense of confidence—but also insecurity. Since potential is measured by a set criteria, falling below that criteria can put one's very intelligence or value at stake.

I recall believing I was smart and questioning that belief after getting low scores on the verbal section of the SAT. If I had allowed those scores to define my potential, I certainly would not be an author today! When we allow our potential to be limited by grades or performance reviews, it affects our belief in our own possibilities.

Many women are trained to operate in this mindset from childhood on. You were praised for your giftedness. This praise may even, at times, have made you feel more special or worthy than others. You probably don't like to admit this, but for many it is true. Parents sometimes even encourage this belief in the name of building confidence in their children. But it is dangerous. What happens when you believe the reason you succeed is solely based on your giftedness? When you don't succeed, it can be devastating. You are constantly in a position of proving how smart you are and how gifted you are. And the pressure can be intense. So much so that people with a fixed mindset shy away from challenges they are unsure they can conquer. "Better to stay in my comfort zone than to risk failure," they say to themselves subconsciously. Every opportunity or challenge is an evaluation of their worth. "Will I be a success or a failure? Will I gain more approval or end up rejected?"

Another trait of those with a fixed mindset is that they look down on effort. "If you have to try hard, you must not really be that good," the fixed mindset says. Before I became aware of the mindsets, I discovered this attitude in myself. It was holding me back tremendously and I didn't even know it. The same could be true for you.

Using the technique of coaching through journaling, I began

peeling back the layers as I sought to understand why I was so stuck as I tried to move toward some exciting goals that I'd set for myself. Here's how that internal conversation went:

Question: What am I so afraid of when it comes to being more assertive about marketing my company and services?

Self: I don't know that I am afraid. It just seems like if my marketing is effective, I wouldn't have to directly ask for opportunities.

Question: What is so bad about directly asking for opportunities?

Self: I know it is a normal part of business to ask. And a lot of people ask for opportunities. But if you are really successful and talented, you don't have to ask. You are asked. You are invited.

This was a bit of a lightbulb moment! I was actually surprised to hear myself say this. "Successful people don't have to ask." Where did I get this idea from? I knew I believed it, but I also knew it might be a faulty belief. So I continued probing. This is what you have to do sometimes to get to the bottom of an issue. Without having a name for it at the time, what I discovered was a fixed mindset. Here's what I was really saying: *If you have talent, you don't have to try so hard. You don't have to ask! Trying hard somehow diminishes your talent. You aren't really that talented if the way you arrived at success was by putting forth so much effort. Gifted people are naturally successful.* So I continued the self-coaching conversation:

Question: So is it true that successful people—truly successful ones—don't have to ask? Think of highly successful people you know. Is this the principle they subscribe to?

Self: Well, as I think about my mentors and even well-known entrepreneurs, I know they ask for opportunities. They don't just wait to see what shows up. They get clear about what they want and they are not afraid to ask for it.

Question: So is your belief that "successful and talented people don't ask" helping you or hurting you?

Self: It's definitely hurting me. First, it's simply untrue. And second, it's leading me to use an approach that is much too passive.

Question: What new belief do you want to replace that old one with?

Self: Truly successful people ask for opportunities. They don't just market, they also sell. And they put forth a lot of effort, which in no way diminishes their talent. Instead, it shows their commitment. Not asking because you believe it will diminish your talent is simply prideful.

In this short five-minute self-coaching exercise, I unearthed a limiting belief that had been lying just beneath the surface of my actions (or lack thereof) for years. And it was rooted in a fixed mindset that says effort is somehow a negative. After all, if you fail and you can say you didn't really put forth much effort, you have an excuse. But if you fail and you truly gave it your all, your very worth is at stake. Women with a fixed mindset are terrified of failure. In the mind of a woman with a fixed mindset, failure is not what you do, but it defines who you are. The exciting part is that you have a choice.

Think back to a time when you failed and then called into question your own intelligence or abilities. Perhaps you began to doubt whether you could ever accomplish what you set out to do. You failed in a relationship and decided you were doomed to remain single forever. "I just don't get the love thing. I'm no good at it," you say. Or, "I keep getting rejected by men. I must be unlovable." These are decisive evaluations of your relationship abilities that give you no room for improvement. "This is who you are and how you are and it's not going to change," the fixed mindset says. That mindset works just fine when you are succeeding at everything, but when you start struggling or failing, it simply leaves no hope for the future.

The fixed mindset says life dealt you a hand and that's it. This often causes people, dissatisfied with the hand they've been dealt, to bluff about the hand they've been given. These are people who often feel afraid they will be found out. They are constantly trying to prove themselves and sometimes feel like an imposter putting on a façade of smarts and personality to win people's approval and praise. The growth mindset offers an approach that melts anxiety and opens the door to amazing possibilities. It says your natural traits are more than just something you have to live with, but simply a starting point. You can cultivate the qualities needed to succeed through your own efforts. A growth mindset believes you can grow through experience and change substantially through your actions. Unlike a fixed mindset, a growth mindset doesn't disdain effort. It thrives on it!

Because those with a growth mindset believe that through effort they can learn things they previously did not understand, improve personality traits, and even grow in intelligence, they are not as easily discouraged by failure. When you have a growth mindset, challenges that stretch you far beyond your comfort zone actually excite you. You realize you're going to *learn* something. You will be expanded by the experience, not judged by it.

Women with a growth mindset believe that with years of discipline and passion, their true potential is unknown. Why waste time hiding your shortcomings rather than simply overcoming them? Why not make friends or search for a spouse who will challenge you to grow rather than simply quell your insecurities? Why stay in your comfort zone and play it safe when you could stretch toward your true dreams?

Another important distinction is this: Studies show that just as people are very poor predictors of what will make them truly happy, we are also poor judges of our own abilities. Those who are most inaccurate at estimating what they are capable of are those with a fixed mindset.

Consider this: If you believe you can improve, you are not as intimidated by the idea that your abilities are not currently as great as you would like. In your mind, those abilities are not set in stone. They will change as you actively learn and grow. However, if you believe that your abilities are permanently set you will be more likely to inflate them. If there's no room for growth or change, you'll want to impress people as much as possible right now!

DOES A GROWTH MINDSET NEGATE STRENGTHS?

When you build on your strengths rather than assuming they are fixed, you multiply your efforts. Sure, you may be a natural-born leader and you've been leading for years, but does that mean you couldn't still be more effective? A woman with a fixed mindset is content to rest on her laurels. A growth mindset sees strengths as only a starting point. Wisely, she taps into her strengths and then nourishes that talent.

Choosing a growth mindset doesn't mean your individual strengths don't matter. In fact, a woman with a growth mindset notices strengths and weaknesses more than those with a fixed mindset. It simply recognizes that skills can be developed—whether in one's career, relationships, finances, spiritual life, or health habits.

This is particularly exciting news if you have ever felt you were stuck with your circumstances—that your intelligence is a fixed entity, that your relationship skills are set, or that your penchant for flubbing finances is an unchangeable trait you inherited from a parent. You *can* change. You are capable of far more than you may have previously thought.

Dream of changing careers, but feel like it's too late to change course? Always wish that you had gone to college or graduate school, but fear you can't cut it? Had a string of broken relationships and feel like you'll never understand the opposite sex? There is abundant hope for you! You can learn new skills, patterns, and habits that will transform your ability to succeed at the endeavors most meaningful to you. Your most successful path to doing so will marry your strengths with a growth mindset—taking you to higher heights than you've ever experienced before.

It's time to stretch beyond your comfort zone.

I learned this firsthand after uncovering my fixed mindset belief that successful women somehow "ascend" to the top. They don't have to ask for opportunities. Instead, if they are really talented, opportunities show up on their own. To be clear, opportunities often do show up on their own for women with talent. They are a like a magnet that attracts opportunities. But there can sometimes be a strategic danger to using "attraction" as your sole method of success. What happens when you don't attract the right opportunities? What happens when you want to go to a completely new level and you are simply not in the right place or around the right types of people to bring that vision to fruition? What happens if God is calling you out of your comfort zone to stretch and break free of your fear of rejection or failure? It is during those times that it is essential to tap into a growth mindset.

In fact, it could be argued that God calls us to a growth mindset. Consider these Scriptures:

- "Do not conform to the pattern of this world, but be transformed by the renewing of your mind."—Romans 12:2

- "With God, all things are possible."—Matthew 19:26

- "To him who is able to do immeasurably more than all we ask or imagine, according to his power that is at work within us."—Ephesians 3:20

From a spiritual perspective, you cannot possibly believe that your potential is fixed and has no potential to expand. If you believe all things are possible, then you can rest assured that if you open your mind, you could find yourself growing beyond your wildest dreams.

Have you told yourself that you're stuck in any of these areas? Where do you believe you have little hope or no further potential?

- *Presentation skills.* You are scared to death to speak in front of people. You've accepted this, and, for the most part, avoid any situation in which you are asked to make a presentation.

- *Accounting and finance.* You don't know the difference between a financial statement and a balance sheet, and see no reason to fix that. You've decided you're not that good with numbers and you can live with that. When people talk finances in a meeting, your motto is from Proverbs 17:28: "Even fools are thought wise if they keep silent!"

- *Personal finances.* Maybe you never find yourself in a situation where you need to understand business accounting, but you cannot avoid the need to better manage your personal finances. You are financially illiterate and don't understand what it will take for you to ever find financial freedom and peace. And the idea of learning scares you.

- *Getting fit.* You see women in magazines or even jogging down the street who seem to have some magical ability to take care of themselves. You were never an athlete as a kid, and see no reason to start now. The idea of making fitness a part of your lifestyle—something that you do daily—seems daunting and out of character for you. Yet it is also intriguing. Could you actually do it?

- *New career.* You don't actually want to be in pharmaceutical sales or teaching or _____ (you fill in the blank!) any more. You have a dream of becoming an attorney or author or _____. But do you really have what it takes? You don't know anything about the field—you just know you feel drawn to it and you have the strengths for it. Is that enough to take a step in a new direction? There's so much you'd have to learn. What if you can't cut it?

- *Love life.* You and your husband seem to be stuck in a rut. He just doesn't get you. He probably never will. And frankly, you're so frustrated with him that you've given up trying to see his point of view or to keep bending and changing to please him. After twelve years of marriage, you have almost lost hope that this will ever be the kind of marriage you'd dreamed of before you tied the knot. Now you just feel stuck.

Is there really hope for undoing old habits? Could you actually learn to communicate better?

- *Shyness.* You've always been shy. It's the reason you don't have many friends, and you blame your lack of career advancement on it. After all, shy people aren't exactly good networkers. Shyness is a personality trait, right? That's not something you can change. Well, what if you could?

That's the question I want to plant as a seed in your mind. What if you could change? What if being shy or a procrastinator or a poor communicator or math-averse was something you could permanently overcome? If there was a road map to doing so, would you be willing to follow the map? I hope so. Open your mind to the possibility that what you know now as your potential is only a fraction of what is truly possible. The key to advancement is recognizing that your limitations are not unchangeable, fixed, or genetic. With education you can expand your understanding in these areas. With discipline, your possibilities are truly limitless.

HOW DO YOU EXPLAIN SUCCESS?

At the beginning of the chapter we examined your perceptions of a recent failure. Your success is determined just as much by your thinking style as your failures. Think back to a recent success you had. It can be something big or small. Jot it down here:

_____

_____

_____

_____

_____

Why did you succeed? Jot down a few bullet-pointed reasons here:

_____

Now, let's take a look at how you explain your success. Did you attribute it to external factors (luck, other people, the weather) or internal ones (you worked hard, you're smart, you're disciplined)? Did you see your success as temporary (I succeeded this time, but who knows if I can pull it off again?) or permanent (it could definitely happen again)? Did you see it as specific (I am good at this one thing, and that's it) or pervasive (my success at this task represents a bigger theme in my life)?

DO YOU EXPLAIN
YOUR SUCCESS AWAY?

Interestingly, a disproportionate number of women who succeed at high levels experience what researchers call the "imposter syndrome." It is a phenomenon that occurs when you are unable to really connect the dots and internalize your accomplishments. Despite your hard work, competence, and experience, you see success as a fluke, pure luck, or your ability to get others to believe you are smarter or more talented than you really are. As a result, you have a nagging feeling that people are going to find you out—that eventually, the jig will be up and you'll be found out. Strangely, successful men simply do not report feeling this way nearly as often as women. I recall a coaching client whose successful talent had been showcased nationally, even landing her on the Oprah Winfrey Show. She confided to me, "I feel like a fraud. I mean, I do the work, but I don't think I'm more talented than anyone else. I always feel like people are going to find out that I'm really not that great." A recent *Psychology Today* article pointed out rich and famous women who were impacted by the imposter syndrome. After being nominated for three Academy awards and six Golden Globes, actress

Michelle Pfeiffer shared her self-doubts in an interview in 2002. "I still think people will find out that I'm really not very talented. I'm really not very good. It's all been a big sham." The article went on to quote Academy Award winner Kate Winslet: "Sometimes I wake up in the morning before going off to a shoot, and I think, I can't do this. I'm a fraud."

If it happens at such public and high levels of success, what happens to us in the everyday efforts of life—in our marriages and relationships, as mothers and managers, employees and business owners? Whether you face doubts as severe as feeling like a fraud or occasionally doubt yourself in the face of a particularly difficult challenge, the key is to notice what you say to yourself about your success. True success is not anxious or doubtful, but confident and at peace. If you find that a pessimistic thinking style is invading your thoughts, you have the power to renew those thoughts by choosing a new outlook.

BUILD SELF-AWARENESS

So what does this all mean for you? When you succeed, even in the small things, you want your thinking style to be the opposite of when you fail.

When you succeed, attribute it to:	When you fail, attribute it to:
Internal factors	External factors
See it as permanent rather than temporary	See it as temporary rather than permanent
See it as pervasive rather than specific	See it as specific rather than pervasive

In his book *Learned Optimism*, Dr. Martin Seligman notes, "Some people, the ones who give up easily, habitually say of their misfortunes: 'It's me, it's going to last forever, it's going to undermine everything I do.' Others, those who resist giving in to misfortune, say: 'It was just circumstances, it's going away quickly anyway, and besides, there's much more in life.'"*

---

* Martin E.P. Seligman, *Learned Optimism* (New York: Vintage Books, 2006).

What does this all mean for you? As you navigate the path to your life's vision, pay attention to your thoughts. Refuse to allow pessimistic thinking to rule. Sure, pessimistic thoughts may invade your mind. But intentionally question those thoughts, and ensure that the thoughts you embrace are accurate and productive. In other words, any thoughts that produce self-sabotaging fear and paralyze you from moving forward need to be rejected. It is a choice. With practice, it is a choice you will make more quickly over time. You will develop an optimistic thinking style that empowers you to dream bigger, bolder dreams and walk into your vision with confidence. And you will be empowered to cut through the fears and excuses that threaten to hold you back. By intentionally noticing your thoughts and questioning the counterproductive ones, you will cultivate an optimistic thinking style that will propel you to the next level.

FOUR QUESTIONS
TO CONQUER EXCUSES

What's the reason you have for not pursuing your most authentic dream? Whatever that dream is in your life or career, you probably have a reason it hasn't happened yet. But if you look behind the reasons, you might just discover that they could be reclassified as excuses—thoughts you are embracing that sabotage your dreams. Excuses are born of a pessimistic thinking style and fixed mindset. Now, I'm not trying to beat you up about your excuses. I want to help you break free of them so you can go to the next level. Whatever you want to call them—excuses or reasons—they're in the way. And *you* are the only one who can demand they go.

So what's your excuse? Is it a lack of time? Money? Is it that person who is always tearing you down? Is the dream just too hard? Too complex? Too much of a commitment? Maybe your excuse is a lack of education or experience. Or perhaps if you just had more contacts or more friends or fewer obligations or weighed less or…

You get my point. Excuses allow us to justify our lack of progress. They can even bring you sympathy. They let you off the hook. But the truth is, when there is something you were meant to do, you'll never truly be off the hook. You *must* do it, which means you must let go of your excuses. That means facing your fear—whether it is fear of success and all the expectations that come with it or fear of failure and all the disappointment or embarrassment that come with it.

Whatever your fear, the good news is that you can muster the courage to conquer it. Choose to let go of all excuses for why you cannot have what you want in life. Coach yourself with these four excuse-shattering questions:

1. What's my excuse?

2. What does this excuse give me permission to do (or not do)?

3. If I could no longer use this excuse, what would I have to do instead?

4. Why don't I just do that now?

When you drop your excuses, you discover that the bottom line is you can choose to pursue your dreams—or not. You can live life fully or you can live it small. Living fully takes courage. Courage is a choice. The choice is yours.

WHAT ARE YOU HOPING FOR?

What is it that you are hoping for? What's that thing that caused you to pick up this book in the first place? There is something you haven't yet experienced, but want to. There is something that represents that gap between where you are right now and where you want to be. And the first step to you closing that gap is believing two simple words: It's possible. Just say that out loud right now: "It's possible." Your dream is possible. With the right thoughts, the right actions, and the right relationships, whatever divine dreams rest in your heart are possible.

So as you begin this journey, this first step is about hope. You must have it. Hope is the foundation of faith and the essence of optimism. When you stop hoping, you start settling. As I coach women in particular, and as I reflect on my own personal experience, I have noticed how often people downsize their dreams. Women so often attempt to juggle multiple roles and responsibilities. Many downsize their dreams for so long that settling for less becomes a habit. Can you relate? *When you stop hoping, you start settling.* You begin to settle for a smaller version of your real vision. What have you stopped hoping for out of fear that you won't get it? In what ways has "settling" crept in and buried a hope for something better?

Coach You:
What do you need to give yourself permission to hope for?

Give yourself permission to hope again. To dream a bigger dream. Successful women are confident enough to dream authentic dreams. It means you have to be honest enough with yourself to acknowledge the real desires of your heart. No time for surface goals. No time for putting everyone else's agenda ahead of God's plan for you. Be bold and courageous about what you are hoping for. I'm asking you to stretch and see beyond your current circumstances and resources. Reach toward the heavens and trust that although your divine destiny lies beyond your reach, God can close that gap by meeting you more than halfway. It's that kind of believing that requires faith.

As life brings disappointment or failures, it can be tempting to stop hoping for some of the things you truly want. If you're not hoping for anything, you don't need faith. So what is it that you need to start hoping for? What is it that you've hesitated to admit is the real vision for your life? I believe you are reading these words because *now is the time* to start dreaming bigger. Now is the time for a new season of confidence and passion and purpose.

I dare you to dream a bigger dream, and refuse to give up hope.

I'm not talking about cherishing false expectations that set you up for heartache and disappointment. I'm talking about renewing the goals, desires, and visions that speak to you deep within your spirit. Hope energizes you. It inspires. It motivates. Sometimes you don't get what you hope for right when you want it, but if you stop hoping altogether, you cease to take the actions that will bring your dreams to life.

Perhaps author Joyce Meyer summed it up best: "I feel that if I believe for a lot and get even half of it, I am better off than I would be to believe for nothing and get all of nothing."

Be true to your desires by giving yourself permission to hope for something more. And most importantly, *believe* you can do it. Believing that you have what it takes is the first habit of success.

YOUR BEST POSSIBLE FUTURE SELF

Research indicates that imagining your best possible future self is a powerful exercise. Much of the thrill of changing your mindset to move to a new level of success is becoming the kind of woman who can break through fears, navigate obstacles, and believe that with God all things are possible. *All* things are possible. You don't have to know how. But you do have to believe. That's hope. That's optimism. Starting today, make it your goal to cultivate optimism as a success strategy.

Every Woman Should Know

- Optimists live longer, on average, than pessimists—by as much as nine years.

- Depression has been described as the "ultimate pessimism." Women with an optimistic thinking style tend to fend off depression when bad events occur. The opposite is true for those with a pessimistic thinking style.

- In career fields such as teaching, sales, litigation, and public relations, optimism is a predictor of success.

PERSONAL COACHING TOOLKIT: POWER QUESTIONS TO ENHANCE YOUR THINKING STYLE

Answer each of these questions in a journal or with a coach or friend who can listen objectively and give you the space to explore your answers without attempting to *give* you the answers.

1. Spend some time in meditation. The perfect dream for you is the one God uniquely equipped you for. Paint a picture of what the next level of success looks like for you. What is your *real* dream (not the downsized one)?

2. What would it mean to you to be able to accomplish that dream? Picture yourself living that vision. What does it feel like?

3. What gifts, talents, passions, or experiences will you draw on to reach your goal?

4. Think back to a time when you were at your best and reached a particularly meaningful goal. How did you do it? What did you learn about yourself?

5. Consider that meaningful goal you described in the last question. What enabled you to be at your best? Who were the people, circumstances, and other key factors surrounding your success?

6. How could you go about recreating similar circumstances to empower you to reach that "next level of success" you described in the first question?

7. Think back to a time when you failed to reach a goal. What personal factor(s) led you to fail? What external factor(s) led you to fail? What lesson(s) can you glean from these contributing factors to help you succeed when reaching future goals?

8. Realistically, when you look at the picture you painted in the first question, what are the most significant obstacles you might face? If you don't know, take a look at role models who have already been where you aim to go and pinpoint the obstacles they faced.

9. How can you reduce the risk of those obstacles occurring as you move forward? How will you navigate around those obstacles if they occur?

10. Describe your best possible future self. Who is she and how does she approach life?

Think Differently

Be intentional about what you say to yourself when you fail as well as when you succeed. Choose hope. Dream big. Learn new skills. Believe all things are possible.

Get off the Hedonic Treadmill

———— ✳ ————

*Why we are poor predictors of our own
happiness and how you can get it right*

Key Lessons:

- Women, on average, are less happy today than 40 years ago
- Develop the ability to be content while also aiming higher
- Tailor your own personal happiness program

E ver experienced the excitement of a new car—the smell, the beauty, the new gadgets—only to have it wear off a few months later after you get used to it? Or moved into a new place—one much nicer than your previous residence—but within a short time become accustomed to bigger closets or extra space? Worse yet, have you ever left one situation—such as a job or relationship—only to find yourself in a new one with equally stressful challenges?

Terrie was determined not to be like her mother—a housewife who struggled to make ends meet when Terrie's father left their family after falling in love with his administrative assistant. Terrie was ten when her parents divorced, and now, 25 years later, she finally realized how many of her choices had been about proving she didn't need a man to make it in the world. She attended a terrific college and earned a graduate degree to boot. She had, in essence, provided everything for herself that her father did not—and more. In twelve years she bought three homes, "trading up" each time —first a condo, then a small bungalow near downtown, and now a 3,000 square foot house in the suburbs. Her widowed sister and nephew came to live with her after she bought the last home, so she at least had some company. It was an awful lot of space for one person. A new car was a necessity and she never kept one longer than two and a half years. She filled her life with stuff—expensive stuff. It gave her comfort to know she could afford it on her own.

However, it was never enough. The newness always wore off and Terrie soon needed something better to feel good. By the time Terrie came to me for coaching, she knew her penchant for new and better stuff was leaving her feeling unfulfilled and draining her bank account. What she wanted was *happiness*. How she went about finding happiness, however, delivered only temporary bursts of it—fleeting pleasure, not lasting joy.

Happiness is a great motivator. Most things we pursue in life—jobs, relationships, money—we pursue because we believe they will bring happiness. So isn't it critical to know what actually does? The fact is, we have more food, cars, and clothes, better health, double the income, bigger houses, and more conveniences than we had 50 years ago, but those in developed nations like the United States, Britain, and Japan are no happier.* In fact, once a person has enough income to live on, making them happier can be quite a challenge unless they gain the wisdom to understand what really matters.

We think we know what makes us happy. So we strive for it, even chase after it. Often, we get it. And then we get used to it. Boredom or discontentment sets in and we declare that there's something more we need in order to be happy. Welcome to what psychologists call the "hedonic treadmill"—the process of continually adapting to improving circumstances and eventually returning to a relatively neutral point.

Part of the problem is confusing the event of crossing the finish line with the experience of getting there. You get that new house and you're thrilled, but a couple of years later the thrill is gone. You finally reach that big goal you've been aiming for, but the achievement feels

---

* "World Database of Happiness," Ruut Veenhoven, last modified January 9, 2011, www.world databaseofhappiness.eur.nl.

oddly anticlimactic. The most successful women—those who are fulfilled—have developed the maturity to know what really matters and put the rest in perspective. They don't chase achievements and pleasure-inducing events, but build a foundation for contentment.

James 4:3 warns, "When you ask, you do not receive, because you ask with wrong motives, that you may spend what you get on your pleasures." Getting off the hedonic treadmill means embracing contentment.

There is a paradox about success and happiness: the higher your success level, the higher your expectations. And the higher your expectations, the more opportunity for disappointment. As you probably know from experience, disappointment doesn't exactly fuel happiness. In fact, over the last 30 years the people reported to be the happiest nation in the world are the Danish. They tend to be healthy, married, and physically active—all proven contributors to happiness. But these facts don't tip them over the scales of happiness. Instead, it seems people in Denmark have lower expectations than other Westerners, including their neighbors Finland and Sweden who have a similar culture and climate. Eric Weiner, author of *The Geography of Bliss: One Grump's Search for the Happiest Places in the World*, said this in a New York Times article about happiness and expectations:

> Yes, happiness is a function of our expectations—or, as it has been said: "Happiness equals reality minus expectations." Given that neat formulation, there are two ways to attack the problem: boost our reality or lower our expectations. Most of us choose the former. We'd rather stew in our misery than trim our expectations. Lowering our sights smacks us as a cop out, un-American. Better a nation of morose overachievers, we reason, than a land of happy slackers.*

So what's a woman to do? Lower her expectations? Stop dreaming big to keep from being disappointed? You may have figured out by now that I'd never tell you to stop dreaming and believing. But I will tell you this: if you want true success, the kind that creates a harmony

---

* Eric Weiner, "Lowered Expectations," *New York Times*, July 19, 2009.

of purpose, resilience, and joy, you will have to develop the ability to be content while also aiming higher.

Being grateful for your many blessings while believing more is possible is a sign of spiritual maturity. It will require you to let go of the guilt of asking God for more. There should be no guilt, after all, if your primary mission is about service. You getting more, then, also means that others get more. Ask and expect with the right motives and you will demonstrate the kind of stewardship that leads to greater opportunities. "You have been faithful with a few things; I will put you in charge of many things," Jesus says in the parable of the talents (Matthew 25:23). However, when your motives are impure—about simply accumulating accolades, achievements that are not purposeful, or material possessions—it will be impossible to find contentment. You will always want more because the thrill of victory, no matter how great, will eventually wear off.

This is why studies show that we are poor predictors of what will make us happy. Time and again, we proclaim, "If only I had X, I would be happy" or "If only I could *do* X, I would be happy." However, when we get X or do X, we soon find ourselves saying the same thing—but this time instead of X, it's Y.

We have to start by getting clear about what really matters. Let's take a moment to boost our knowledge and understanding of what is known to actually make us happier, and to understand why, as women, happiness seems elusive at times.

WHY IS WOMEN'S HAPPINESS ON THE DECLINE?

Betsey Stevenson and Justin Wolfers, professors at the famed Wharton School at the University of Pennsylvania, released a surprising study that has garnered a great deal of attention. "The Paradox of Declining Female Happiness," as the study is called, indicated that although the lives of American women have improved in numerous ways since the 1970s, women's overall happiness has declined both absolutely and relative to men. In fact, in the 1970s women reported higher levels of happiness than men, but today that gender gap has reversed. Men are happier—and appear to get happier with age—while women, after about the age of 40, become less happy. Why is this? And what changes can you make to your life to keep from mirroring these statistics?

Our incomes have increased. Opportunities are far more abundant. Women's educational achievements have not only increased, but actually surpassed those of men. Housework is not as cumbersome, due to advances in technology. However, some would argue that the increased opportunities have also led to increased amounts of *work*—both paid and unpaid. Many women work a famous "second shift," and while the average man certainly does more household work today than he did forty years ago, some researchers point out that women maintain an "emotional responsibility" that men do not. Working women tend to feel a greater pressure than working men, feeling both responsible for and judged by their success in domestic matters—a clean home, well-behaved children, and so forth. Working women feel that they are expected to uphold the same standards as women who devote themselves full-time to homemaking, even while knowing that it's unreasonable to expect to accomplish so much.

Men, from a cultural standpoint, have never been measured against an expectation of staying at home and caring for children. A man is trained to find a profession in which he can excel and provide for his family. Consider for a moment the cultural reaction to a single man whose home is in disarray, who never cooks, and has little aptitude for raising children. It is almost sympathetic: "Oh, poor thing, he just needs to find a good wife."

Now imagine a single woman with similar characteristics—a messy home, rarely cooks, and has yet to give a second thought to having children. Culturally, she is judged more harshly. Women are expected to excel domestically. So even in equitable marriages in which spouses share the responsibilities of cooking, cleaning, and childrearing, women feel societal pressure to measure up to expectations in a way that men simply do not experience.

Along these lines, a recent study of professional women showed they experience much higher levels of guilt than men when work intrudes on home life. Men felt little guilt when receiving phone calls at home after hours or responding to work-related e-mail or text messages. Women, however, are more likely to feel guilty. The study, which was published in the *Journal of Health and Social Behavior* and conducted by researchers at the University of Toronto, analyzed information from more than 1,000 American workers. Interestingly, levels of guilt were consistent among women regardless of age, marital status, parental status, or socioeconomic level—and the more frequently they experienced work contact at home, the more guilty they felt. The study's coauthor, Scott Schieman, suggests that the differences between men's response to work intrusions to personal time and women's response is due to differing expectations about the boundaries between home and work. "These forces may lead some women to question or negatively evaluate their family role performance when they're trying to navigate work issues at home," Schieman says.

Our lives are also more complex than forty years ago, and overall happiness is reflected in multiple domains of life. The question of happiness today revolves around more than just how things are going at home. It may also reflect what is happening on the job and the juggling of work and home responsibilities. In essence, with more opportunities come more chances for failure. A pessimistic view, perhaps, but true. Can you relate? Most of us today are multitasking multiple responsibilities in multiple areas of life, and it's demanding. It really isn't all that hard to drop the ball in one or two areas when there are so many options to choose from!

There is one interesting caveat to all of this research that is worth noting: happiness levels for black women have *increased* over the same period of time. This is the only group of women for whom this is true. Similar trends in increased income, education, and opportunities have occurred for black women. However, the starting point is not similar. In large numbers, African-American women were already primarily working outside the home while raising families long before the 1970s. As a result, the improvement of opportunities in areas such as income, job opportunities, and education may have impacted overall happiness as well as decreases in overt racial prejudice compared to 40 years ago.

No one knows for sure what the reasons are, but women overall throughout the industrialized world have seen declining levels of happiness over the last four decades. It is impossible to discuss success without talking about happiness. Remember that our definition of success for the purposes of this book is living your life's purpose while embracing joy and resilience as you do. It is described as a harmony of service, achievement and *happiness*. What is success if you cannot enjoy it?

REDEFINING SUCCESS FOR YOURSELF

So how do you define success for yourself? Will you be successful when you get a certain title at work? Make a certain amount of money? Get married? Have a baby? Finally buy your dream home? The truth is that success looks different for each of us, but to find true happiness, you need to define success by what holds real meaning in life—relationships, making a difference, and living an authentic life, for starters. Those who chase after the next best thing are rarely satisfied, finding themselves on that never-ending hedonic treadmill. They find short-term thrills only to be let down once the newness wears off. Consider these five ways to define success on your own terms:

1. *Value fulfillment more than success.* Success, especially in our culture, is often defined by the external—money, job, titles, and possessions. Fulfillment is about living with purpose, using your strengths, and tapping into your passions. Follow your dreams and focus on being in service to others.

2. *Aim for excellence, not success.* If you live in the moment, aiming to be your best and do your best, success will surely follow. The old adage that "success is about the journey, not the destination," holds true. In what ways are you focused on getting to the goal line, but not doing your best on the way there? Start focusing on being your best in each moment and with each step, and the sense of fulfillment and accomplishment that follows will leave no room for regrets.

3. *Measure success by your own standards, not society's.* Get specific. At this stage of your life, how do you define success? Consider the five key areas of your life—relationships, work,

finances, health, and spirituality. Identify one measure in each area that will let you know you are succeeding. For example, "praying together as a family every day" might be a spiritual measure, "saving 15 percent of my income" might be a financial measure, and "doing work I love" could be a measure of success at work. Take a moment to jot down your specific measures of success right now.

4. *Ask, "What's my impact?"* One indicator of success is making a positive difference in the world. Serving in some way is the greatest thing we can do. "Everybody can be great because anybody can serve," Martin Luther King, Jr. once said. By focusing on serving, you will live a life of meaning and purpose—knowing that what you do daily makes a positive difference in the world. How is someone's life better because he or she has crossed your path?

5. *Ask, "Is my success making me a better person?"* If you learn from the mistakes along the way and persevere through the tough times, your journey to success will ultimately make you a better person. When you face obstacles or disappointments on your journey, do you get bitter or better?

BUILDING A LIFESTYLE OF HAPPINESS

Knowing what will make you happy is of no use unless you start making choices that set you up for a lifestyle of happiness. This can mean making some big, bold choices. Business leader Cookie Lee is a great example of that.

I had the opportunity to meet Cookie when her company, Cookie Lee Jewelry, invited me to serve as the closing keynote speaker at its annual convention in Las Vegas. Company culture often builds from the top down, so it was obvious months before I met Cookie in person that she was an enthusiastic, energetic leader. To prepare for my keynote, I spoke to the training director, the company CEO (Cookie's husband), and several directors and consultants—all of whom had a contagious enthusiasm about the company, its mission, and their role in it.

Born Debra Lee in 1955, her husband, John, started calling her "Cookie" and the name stuck. She is an ABC, as she describes it—American-born Chinese—and grew up with very high parental expectations about what she would do with her life. "It was the 1960s and many moms in Alameda County, California, where I grew up, were stay-at-home moms, but mine wasn't," Cookie remembers. "My mom worked 8 to 5 and could never go to anything. I knew I wanted to be home with my kids [when I became an adult]," she says. After attending UC Berkeley and then graduating from UC Davis, Cookie went on to graduate school. She earned her MBA from Northwestern University in 1982, which, at the time, was the top school for business and marketing.

She began her career with Johnson & Johnson, working with the company's Tylenol group before being hired as marketing manager for Orville Redenbacher and then Revlon/Max Factor in Los Angeles. "It was glamorous and fun," she remembers. But her plans as a little girl still lingered: she wanted to stay at home with her kids when she became a mom. "I asked myself how I could do that," she says. "For a while, I was painting t-shirts and I realized I wasn't going to be able to do that on a large scale." She didn't have children yet, but she and John planned to. She was determined to be able to have a career and be at home with them when the time finally came.

You can often find purpose from past experiences that shaped you. For Cookie, growing up with a mom working outside the home taught her that she wanted to work at home. So in 1985, after taking a jewelry-making class, she decided to use her marketing skills to launch a business. "The first year I sold $8,000 worth of my jewelry while I was working my corporate marketing job," she recalls. And from there, she always saw a progression in her business. "I am the kind of person who always sees the possibilities and how to get better," she says. "There was a seven-year period where I was growing all by myself," she explains of her then one-woman business. "I chose to do this. I thought it was fun. I was having a good time."

Simultaneously, she was progressing in her corporate career too. By 1989, she left Revlon and was hired by Mattel, the toy company. "By day I would go to work, and at night I would do my business," she says. "I was risk averse!" Cookie developed a business model whereby she sold her jewelry directly to customers through home shows and office shows. "I was doing about 20 shows per month, selling while I was holding down a full-time job. My benchmark was to be able to pay half my mortgage every month. When I reached that point, I knew I would be ready to go full-time in the business."

She exceeded her goal before she made the full-time leap. "By 1990, I brought in $80,000 in sales for Cookie Lee and I was making over $100,000 in my corporate job," she remembers. "I finally realized there are only 24 hours in a day and I'm only one person. The only way for me to grow was to duplicate myself or wholesale my products to retailers, but that would mean being away from home." Cookie made the entrepreneurial leap in perfect timing. Her first child, a boy named Steven, was born in 1991. A year later she gave birth to a daughter, Katie.

"We are a women's company," Cookie says. "We are a family company that is pro-family." She exemplifies that harmony of service, achievement, and happiness that defines true success. "You have to have your 'why'," she says. "For me, my 'why' was that I wanted to be there for my kids no matter what while earning a living and having fun!" That was her mission. "Wanting to drive a Mercedes and be rich is not enough to get off the sofa and stay motivated," she warns. "You have to be very resourceful." She suggests you ask yourself what your *why* is. "Is it to be self-reliant and stand on your own two feet? It must be very personal and you must believe in your mission."

Cookie went full-time with the business in 1991 and her husband, John, joined her in the business in 1992. To grow the business she had to answer some tough questions. "I wanted to maximize my efforts. I always ask myself, 'How can I do less work and have a higher payout?'—whether it's jewelry production or cooking with fewer pots so I don't have as many dishes to wash!" That's when they began seeking out sales consultants who could do exactly what Cookie had done for seven years. The rest is history. Today, Cookie Lee Jewelry has more than 30,000 consultants around the country, almost all of them women with a vision similar to Cookie's—to be able to earn money while still working from home and taking care of their families.

"I never thought the company would be as big as it is," Cookie reflected. "I always said, 'Wouldn't it be great if'…and then things would unfold. Wouldn't it be great if we could have a company trip? Wouldn't it be great if we could sell to women all across the nation?"

When asked what her greatest strength is, Cookie says it's enthusiasm. "I think it's contagious! It makes it easy to motivate people. That energy is very powerful." Indeed, "zest, energy, and enthusiasm" are some of the 24 universal strengths identified by Dr. Christopher Peterson, a psychology professor at the University of Michigan and the foremost researcher on personality strengths. Cookie Lee used her strength of enthusiasm and energy to launch and sustain herself and her business during a seven-year startup phase, then propel it to great heights after quitting her day job. That same enthusiastic energy quashes her fear. "When I go after it, whatever 'it' is, I go at it 150 percent! There is no 'we can't do it.' Maybe it will take longer than we thought, but we *can* do it."

She also had to use this strength to attract consultants to launch their own home-based businesses selling Cookie Lee Jewelry. Cookie certainly thinks differently than the average woman, dismissing fear as "something that is usually just in your head." "I don't usually think, 'Oh, I'm going to fail,'" she says. "My motto is *Never give up*. I do what I do because I believe in it and I am willing to do the work. Every season, when we launch a new line, I think, 'This is the best thing!' Then, when it's time to do it all again and design another line, I think, 'So, what are we going to do next?'" It is this attitude of enthusiasm and anticipation, rooted in a passion for helping women and doing something she loves, that has contributed a great deal to her success. This achievement also relies on her can-do spirit. "When people say that they couldn't figure out a problem, I say, 'Well, why not? Have you brainstormed with a friend or mentor or looked on the Internet or read a book?'" In other words, the answer is out there, but you must have the will to find it.

For Cookie Lee, authentic happiness has emerged from this combination of passion, confidence, optimism, and the pursuit of a lifestyle that has given her what she always wanted: to be there for her children as they grew up. I asked her for the best advice she could give to a woman who asked for the secrets of her success, and she left me with the following thoughts:

- If you give, you're going to get. Giving energizes you. Give to those in need.

- Do your best each and every day. When you know you did the best you could, you go to bed happy.

- Take a step forward and use the resources that God has already put in your hands.

- Don't make excuses! If you really, really want it, you won't have a bunch of excuses. If you do, it's a sign that you don't want it badly enough.

- Know your *why*. Pick an area where you are passionate. If you're doing something you don't like, you're in trouble.

- No matter how difficult the task, you can figure it out if you seek the answers.

- Be willing to share and mentor others. There is more than enough business for everyone.

Cookie believes the business is about happiness—whether it is the design team, the staff, the consultants, or the customers. "The women in Cookie Lee feel good about themselves. They are smiling. God has provided. This is really a happy business."

THE PURSUIT OF
AUTHENTIC HAPPINESS

What, then, would make you happier? Think about it. What is within your control that would genuinely add to your level of happiness? Whatever it is, I challenge you to do it. Happiness can literally prolong your life.

Amazingly, the effect of unhappiness on longevity is comparable to that of smoking, according to a recent analysis of 30 scientific studies on happiness. As a society, we all know by now that smoking is dangerous for your health, but have you ever considered that being unhappy could have health consequences? It's time to take your happiness seriously!

For years, I thought of being happy as a fleeting pursuit—a temporary state of being. Spiritually speaking, I believed a more noble aim was to have joy and be content no matter my circumstances. Of course, those are important too. But several years ago, I ran across this Scripture written by the very wise King Solomon in Ecclesiastes 3:12-13: "There is nothing better for people than to be happy and to do good while they live. That each of them may eat and drink, and find satisfaction in all their toil—this is the gift of God."

In other words, be happy in the everyday activities of life. Find satisfaction in your work. Help others. It is a divine gift to be happy when life is a routine. Abraham Lincoln once noted that "Most people are about as happy as they make up their minds to be." If he was right, then happiness is a choice—an approach and an attitude that we choose to carry into our work, our relationships, and our lives.

Happiness, says Richard Layard, author of *Happiness: Lessons from a New Science*, "is supremely important because it is our overall motivational device."* Happiness is the one thing we pursue for its own sake. Pretty much everything else we pursue because we believe it will make us happier—whether a relationship, money, losing weight, changing careers, discovering our life purpose, gaining wisdom, or even eating. I'd even bet it's fair to say you're reading this book because you believe its contents will lead you to something that will make you happier, is that right?

It turns out, though, that we tend to be poor predictors of what will actually make us happy. And I want to park here for a moment. All of us know what it's like to pour your heart and soul into an endeavor, expecting that you'll be happy when you reach the destination. And then, when you cross the finish line and raise your arms in triumph, you'll soon look around and ask, "Is this it?" Have you ever been there? Consider all of these things that culture tells us (and we often tell ourselves) will make us happy:

---

* Richard Layard, *Happiness* (New York: Penguin Press, 2005).

- A new home
- A new car
- A new spouse
- A new outfit, pair of shoes, or gadget
- A college degree
- More money

Believe it or not, research shows that each of these things increases your level of pleasure or short-term happiness. Eventually, though, the newness wears off. You get used to it, and soon you need something more to bring you happiness. Being on this hedonic treadmill means you continually adapt to improving circumstances and always return to a point of relative neutrality. Can you relate? I'm not saying money or a nice home or a college degree is bad. They are, in fact, good. But if you pursue them for the sake of being happy, you may feel disappointed when the effects wear off as you get used to your new level of "success."

ONLY THREE WAYS MONEY
CAN BUY HAPPINESS, LADIES...

It's the age-old question: Can money buy happiness? In theory, we know the answer is no. Yet, many women (and men) pursue it in great expectation, thinking that when they finally get enough of it, they'll be happy. If you get the bigger house, the right car, the right salary, then you can kick up your heels and revel in your success. But researchers have discovered some interesting facts that may challenge your notions about money and happiness. First of all, the less money you have, the more it can impact your happiness when you get more of it. If you make $10,000 and you quadruple your income to $40,000, your life satisfaction will improve significantly. But beyond $40,000, life satisfaction increases only slightly with increases in income.

That's not to say you shouldn't pursue a better salary. Just know some of the factors that allow money to make you happier. These three questions are among the most important:

1. Can I pay my bills?

The biggest predictor of happiness as it relates to money is not how much of it you make, but whether or not you can pay your bills. So focus on widening the gap between your income and expenses. There are three ways to do that—spend less, make more, or do both. If you double your income, then double or triple your expenses, you set yourself up for stress and anxiety. The easier it is to pay your bills, the happier you'll likely be.

Bottom line: Living below your means increases happiness.

2. Do I make more or less than the people around me?

According to studies, if given the option between making $100,000 in a community where everyone else makes $200,000 or making $50,000 in a community where the average person makes $25,000, the majority of people actually choose to make $50,000. Most people are more concerned with making as much or more than their peers than they are with the actual amount they make.

Bottom line: People feel better when they are above average.

3. Do I spend my money making someone else happy?

Not that we needed research to confirm it, but it does: It is better to give than to receive. People report higher levels of happiness when they spend money on others than when they spend it on themselves. There's nothing wrong with spending on yourself, but make it a rule to do something for someone else—just for the joy of it.

STOP COMPARING UP

Another important point of distinction between happy women and unhappy women is how they think about their relative position in society. Upward social comparisons are devastating to your happiness. As I mentioned when it comes to money and happiness, people are happier when they are faring better than the people around them. No one likes to feel that they are somehow lagging behind. But especially in America, there are constant reminders that you need more in order to be happy.

Television is said to have a negative impact on your happiness because it encourages social comparison and skews your perception of your relative position in society. Television has a negative impact on your "perceived position," and therefore is bad for your happiness. In fact, studies have shown 67 percent of Americans have blue-collar jobs, but only 10 percent of TV characters do.* Commercials and advertisements send you this message all day long—suggesting that most people live far above average in terms of material lifestyle. And even if you skip the commercials, the barrage of television programming that is skewed toward unrealistic lifestyles broadens the scope of comparison. Seventy years ago, you had only the people in your general community to benchmark your position in life. Today, you see hundreds of people on a daily basis—via television, magazines, and the Internet—with whom to benchmark your progress. Even more disconcerting, most of those people don't represent any semblance of reality—not even on reality television, where "real" scenarios are scripted and the illusions of wealth and privilege are often helped along with network dollars. Television is plastered with millionaires and programs about them are as popular as ever. Put the word millionaire in a TV show and you'll attract more viewers—*Who Wants to Be a Millionaire? Millionaire Matchmaker. Million-Dollar Listing. Joe Millionaire. Secret Millionaire. How I Made My Millions.* Even as far back as 1982, nearly half of all the characters in primetime social dramas were millionaires. According to research, constantly feeding your mind with television images causes you to overestimate the affluence of other people and causes you to perceive your relative financial position as lower than it actually is. And yes, this makes people less happy.

It would be fair to state, however, that while these points are true for people overall, the impact on women may be even greater. We are not only bombarded with images that suggest the average person has more

---

* Schudson, M. *Advertising, The Uneasy Persuasion* (London: Routledge, 1984).

money and a better job than is actually true. We are also constantly being fed unrealistic images and standards of beauty, motherhood, and work-life balance. The opportunity for upward social comparison is endless in our culture. And if you engage in it and are not intentional about limiting your exposure, you will sabotage your well-being and perhaps even your confidence.

Consider this recent conversation as an example: "It just seems like I should be much further along," a client mentioned as she beat herself up for her perceived lack of progress. "It just feels like everyone else who is doing what I'm doing has things figured out and I just keep stumbling."

"Who is everyone else?" I asked, imagining a collective "they" to whom she compared herself. She paused for a moment, and then started naming some of the most successful people in her field—all with considerably more time invested, and a number of stumbles along the way.

"So…I'm curious," I continued. "Where were 'they' at this stage on their path?"

As she began to think about it, she realized "they" were no further along than she and that the comparisons were causing her to judge herself unfairly.

Embrace this phrase as your mantra: Progress is a process! When you spend too much time comparing yourself to others, you take your eyes off your vision and sow unnecessary seeds of doubt and insecurity.

When you are tempted to compare yourself with others, or condemn yourself for what you have or haven't done, consider these four simple questions to help you be more gentle with yourself and begin embracing the process of progress.

1. Are your expectations realistic?

It is important to expect success, but it is equally important not to set your expectations so high that they are rarely, if ever, met. Dream big! Then give yourself a realistic timeline in which to manifest the dream. One of the biggest reasons people never reach their vision is that they expect it to come to life quickly. Give yourself the time and space to succeed—and measure success by your definition, not everyone else's.

2. How far have you come?

It can be easy to forget that every circumstance is unique. Perhaps you could be further along, but you've had a lot to overcome along the way. Give yourself credit for the progress you've made. Perhaps you struggle in opening up in relationships or communicating with others, but you never saw positive relationships or communication modeled for you growing up. Even though you may not be where you want to be, be grateful for the strides you've made in areas that are difficult. Perhaps your stumbling blocks aren't in relationships, but in your finances, career, or health. Acknowledge your progress.

3. Where are you in the process?

Progress is a process. If you've recently transitioned into a new career or started a business, relationship, or other goal, consider where you are in the process. Be willing to stick with your plan, persevere, and practice patience as you move through the stages of learning and growth along your journey.

4. What are you doing right?

Make a list of what you are doing right. When you lose your focus by making comparisons, it is important to bring to mind your positive actions and attributes. This kind of acknowledgment can be a reality check or an energy boost to get you unstuck and refocused on the things you can control.

Stop making comparisons. When you find yourself comparing yourself to others, whether personally or professionally, make a conscious decision to redirect your focus to what you are doing right. Successful women use social comparison in ways that bolster happiness:

- To notice those who are *less* fortunate and seek ways to give and help them.

- To notice those who are *more* fortunate and feel grateful for the life and blessings currently present in their lives.

- To notice those who are further along on their success journey and find inspiration and lessons in their stories.

You have a "happiness set point"

Perhaps you're thinking, "Look, I'm not a naturally cheery person. Some people are just happier than others." You're right. *Half* right, anyway. According to researcher Sonja Lyubomirsky, author of *The How of Happiness,* about 50 percent of happiness is genetic—your "happiness set point." It's your temperament and it pretty much stays the same your entire life. Some of us come out of the womb with a more positive disposition. These are the kids who are always smiling. Laughter is their norm. Nothing seems to get them down. If you're one of these people, consider yourself fortunate. If not, there's hope—because 40 percent of happiness is about intentional activity. This means that the choices you make and the actions you take have a direct impact on just how happy you are. Happiness is not simply about what happens in your life. It is about what you do, how you think, and the environments you put yourself in. You have control over these factors and if you want to increase the amount of joy and fulfillment in your everyday life, you can do it by taking charge and being intentional.

So if 50 percent of happiness is your temperament and 40 percent is what you do daily, what's the other 10 percent? Interestingly, the findings line up with something the apostle Paul famously said in the book of Philippians: "I have learned to be content whatever the circumstances. I know what it is to be in need, and I know what it is to have plenty. I have learned the secret of being content in any and every situation, whether well fed or hungry, whether living in plenty or in want. I can do all this through him who gives me strength." Just 10 percent of happiness is determined by your circumstances. So why do most of us insist happiness is determined by what happens in life? Such a philosophy leaves you a victim of your circumstances, with little control over emotions. And it points right back to the reason the hedonic treadmill is a never-ending, vicious cycle. Changing your circumstances—whether through a new car, 50-pound weight loss, promotion at work, or winning the lottery—will provide a temporary boost in happiness. But since circumstances account for just 10 percent of happiness, the newness eventually becomes the norm and you revert to your happiness set point. The combination of a set point and intentional activities is so powerful that even in the face of a major setback, such as a disability, people become less happy for awhile, but eventually return to or near their original set point.

What determines happiness?

■ Set point

■ Intentional activity

■ Circumstances

HAPPINESS ACTION PLAN

What, then, is known to boost happiness long-term? First, it is noteworthy that women and men of faith report higher levels of happiness than others. "One of the most robust findings of happiness research: that people who believe in God are happier," says Dr. Richard Layard. "At the individual level one cannot be sure whether belief causes happiness or happiness causes belief. But since the relation also exists at the national level, we can be sure that to some extent belief causes happiness." As a believer, I feel certain it is the latter. But faith is just one component—one that can influence more practical matters.

What you do each day has a direct impact on how you feel. And how you feel, as we will discuss in the next chapter, greatly influences how you make decisions, how long you stick with a goal, and how well you respond to adversity—all key factors in upping your success game. So if you intentionally engage in activities, even simple ones, that are known to impact happiness, you can noticeably increase your happiness levels. Additionally, if you get more knowledge and a better understanding of what *doesn't* make you happier, you can begin to make better choices that build a lifestyle of happiness. "Wisdom is the principal thing; therefore get wisdom. And in all your getting, get understanding," Proverbs 4:7 (NKJV) reminds us.

So what kind of intentional activities should you be doing? It is often the simple acts that are most effective. I've come up with a personal happiness list to help you be intentional about incorporating activities into your life daily that are known to make you happier. Think of this like Weight Watchers for your life.

Aim to complete at least four of the Daily Activities each day to increase your happiness and then maintain it. Engage in one of the Mega Happiness Boosters or Happiness Lifestyle Changes for major shifts or changes that are known to boost well-being. Each of the items listed have been studied and proven to boost positive emotion and increase happiness.

Daily Activities	Mega Happiness Boosters	Happiness Lifestyle Changes
Exercise for 30 minutes (20 or more minutes of exercise can boost your mood for up to 24 hours)	Engage in a gratitude visit (write a letter expressing your gratitude to someone for what they've meant or done in your life. Read it aloud to them—at dinner, in front of friends or family, or alone.)	Transition into a career for which you are passionate
Have six hours or more of social interaction per day (can include phone, e-mail and in-person communication)	Set and reach a meaningful goal	Do work that gives you a sense of making a contribution to the world
Write down three good things that happened today and explain why they were so good to you	Use one or more of your strengths to solve a challenge	Be *happily* married and stay married

Daily Activities	Mega Happiness Boosters	Happiness Lifestyle Changes
Have at least three good belly laughs	Forgive someone for something you are holding on to	Develop and strengthen at least three to four trusting, loving friendships—people you'd consider "confidants"
Participate in some form of volunteer work or do something kind for someone in need	Clear out clutter that's burdening your home and personal space	Get a competent boss who empowers you to use your strengths daily
Meditate for 10 minutes	Take a relaxing vacation, even if it's an at-home "staycation"	Set and reach the goal of living below your means
Get 30 minutes of sunshine	Pinpoint a recent milestone and do something to celebrate	Live in a community where your income is higher than average rather than vice versa
Savor a delicious meal (without multitasking)	Fast from television and other media for one week	Minimize your exposure to television permanently
Sit down to an evening meal with your family and ask, "What's the best thing that happened to you today?"	Spend that extra money on someone else rather than yourself	Live in a city where you have people you truly care about who also care about you
Give a tight hug or kiss to someone you care about	Pamper yourself—light some candles, turn on some relaxing music and take a warm bubble bath	Get involved in your community so you feel truly connected
Get eight hours of sleep tonight	Create a positive portfolio that reminds you of happy times and put it somewhere you'll see it regularly	Get to and stay at a healthy weight

Daily Activities	Mega Happiness Boosters	Happiness Lifestyle Changes
Relish one activity you normally rush through—for example, putting on your makeup, cooking a meal, or taking a shower	Reminisce with a friend or family member about a happy event or memory	Get in the habit of taking pictures of good times and keep an album to help you savor life's treasured moments

As you can see, you can do some of the items on this list right this minute, while others may take more time to accomplish. Make it your goal to incorporate the types of everyday activities into your life that will boost your level of happiness and fulfillment. Don't make it an afterthought. Make it a priority.

Happiness is subjective. No one can tell you how happy you are: you are the sole judge. So doesn't it make sense to get clear about what will truly ignite happiness in your life? I use the word "ignite" because the ingredients for happiness are in your possession right now. Remember the Abraham Lincoln quote I shared earlier? "Most people are about as happy as they make up their minds to be." Make up your mind to be happy! Make the choice to do as Psalm 118:24 instructs: "This is the day the LORD has made; we will rejoice and be glad in it" (NKJV). In doing so, you are making a decision to choose happiness no matter what. Whether or not a goal has been met or a loved one has apologized or the money you need has rolled in, you choose happiness. That means finding something for which to be grateful. It means using what you've got to enjoy your life in this moment. Lighten up. Laugh. Notice the beauty around you. Appreciate the people before you. Look for the opportunity you have today to make a positive difference for someone. Choose today to tap into the divine gifts that have been bestowed upon you. Don't wait. As you use what you've got, you'll see that your happiness is waiting to be uncovered. Too often, we wait for a change that will *make* us happy. Instead, choose to be content no matter the circumstances!

As you build moments of happiness and joy, you will see the power of positive emotion to fuel your perseverance and energy, and you will succeed at higher and higher levels. Positive emotion is a powerful strategy for the high-achieving, resilient woman. For now, all I ask is that you make a decision to live your life in a way that exudes joy. In so doing, your life becomes contagious and creates a ripple effect whose impact you may never fully know.

Every Woman Should Know

- There is a link between altruism and overall longevity. Give back in a tangible way and you'll reap both happiness and health rewards.

- Happy women have stronger immune systems and lower levels of cortisol, the chemical the body produces when under stress.

- Only 10 percent of your happiness is based on circumstances and 40 percent is based on your intentional daily actions.

- Research suggests that happiness actually *causes* more productivity and higher income. So while it is often thought that success causes happiness, it may actually be the other way around.

PERSONAL COACHING TOOLKIT: POWER QUESTIONS TO BOOST YOUR HAPPINESS

Answer each of these questions in a journal or with a coach or friend who can listen objectively and give you the space to explore your answers without attempting to give you the answers.

1. What brings you joy? Make a list. Keep it where you will see it daily when you get up. Then make a decision each morning to incorporate into your day the things that bring you joy.

2. What has a tendency to drain joy from your life? It can be just as important to understand what you *don't* want as it is to know what you *do* want. Find ways to eliminate (and if not possible to eliminate, then at least reduce the effect of) the things that drain your joy.

3. Who are the happy people in your circle of friends? Spend more time talking to and being around happy people. Research is clear that positive friends are a definite happiness booster.

4. When it comes to work-life harmony, what do you feel guilty about? Guilt typically indicates that we think we have done something wrong. Dig a little deeper if you are feeling guilty and ask yourself, "What belief or personal rule am I breaking that causes me to feel guilty? Is this value or rule helping me or hurting me? If it is hurting me, is it time for me to choose a more helpful belief or rule for myself? If so, what is it?"

5. Take a look at the happiness lifestyle changes listed earlier in this chapter. What lifestyle changes do you want to make a personal goal? What will this lifestyle change give you that you do not have right now?

6. Consider the reference to the study *The Paradox of Declining Female Happiness*. What expectations did you hold earlier in your adult life that have not been met? In what ways has this impacted your happiness? What adjustments could you make to those expectations?

7. There is no question that strong relationships contribute to higher levels of happiness. In fact, having three to four very close friendships is shown to have a tremendous influence on your life. Who are your three closest confidants? What could you do to strengthen those relationships? If you do not have three or four very close friends, what steps could you take towards strengthening an existing friendship or meeting new, like-minded people?

8. What is your personal definition of happiness?

9. In what ways do you tend to compare up? When are you triggered to start comparing yourself up? Next time you feel inclined to do so, put things into perspective by also reminding yourself of your tremendous blessings.

10. What can you do today to boost someone else's happiness? Always remember that one of the fastest ways to happiness is serving someone else.

Think Differently:

Be intentional about taking actions daily that lead to authentic happiness.

Stop Trying to Fix Your Weaknesses

———— ✳ ————

*Why you should stop obsessing about what's wrong
with you and start building on what's right*

Key Lessons

- Identify and embrace your strengths
- Find ways to use your strengths to conquer challenges
- Build confidence by only using words that strengthen you, not weaken you. Learn to speak well of yourself.

Reverend Cynthia Hale was a trailblazer of sorts when she answered the call to ministry. She responded to a request from her denomination to start a church—from scratch—just outside Atlanta in Lithonia, Georgia, in the 1980s. She walked away from a secure job as a prison chaplain and an impending promotion to move to Atlanta and take on the challenge of starting a church. She took a 30 percent pay cut. She knew only one person in Atlanta, a theology professor and mentor who introduced her to his family and helped her look around the city.

Her gender was a major hurdle at that time. Some even said it was a weakness in her job. "People liked me and my preaching, but they questioned whether God really called me to do this," Dr. Hale said. She, however, had no doubts about her calling. "God spoke to me in college," she says. "I took a year off after graduation and then headed to Duke University Divinity School."

Using her strength for leadership, she began the church as a Bible study out of her apartment and inspired attendees to engage in what she calls *lifestyle evangelism*. "I met people at the grocery store and the athletic club. One person came and brought several attorneys with him!" she remembers. "Lifestyle evangelism is what Jesus teaches. I literally taught people how to effectively invite people to Bible study and church." By the time they launched the church, they had 80 members. By year four, nearly 500 people joined. In the fifth year, 1,000 people joined Ray of Hope Christian Church, and now they have 2,500 members. She knows she couldn't have done it alone. While her ministry inspired them, it was the strength and outreach of others that built the church. Successful women know they can't go it alone, and they know the importance of filling in the gaps in their own strengths.

Stop focusing on what's wrong and start building on what's right

It is easy to focus on what's wrong with you or others and setting your mind to try to fix it. Many women are wired for finding flaws. Our culture encourages it, in fact! As women, we are bombarded with messages about fixing what's "wrong" with us—whether it's our body shape or hair or skin or mothering skills or housekeeping habits or... you get the picture. If you're not careful, your inner dialogue can begin to sound like the television and magazines that are so good at letting you know what's wrong with you. I want you to be intentional about making a shift from weakness-based personal improvement to strengths-based personal improvement. This is a key to success that is not only empowering, but makes your journey to victory easier and also more fun.

So much of self-help, coaching, and psychology has been about helping people figure out and fix what's wrong with them so that they can finally be more successful. But both Scripture and research show that when you focus on building on your innate strengths rather than fixing your weaknesses, success flows more easily and authentically.

Believe it or not, there is power in being imperfect if you identify and use your unique strengths to overcome your so-called weaknesses.

Esteemed business consultant Peter Drucker said, "The ageless essence of leadership is to create an alignment of strengths in ways that make a system's weaknesses irrelevant." Your weaknesses do not have to become an obstacle to getting what you want in life. In fact, God's strength is perfected in our weakness. Second Corinthians 12:9 (NKJV) promises, "My grace is sufficient for you, for My strength is made perfect in weakness."

WHEN ARE YOU AT YOUR BEST?

Think back to a highpoint or an experience in your life in which you were at your best—whether in a relationship or at work, in your finances or health. What conditions empowered you to be at your best? What character strengths did you tap into? What lessons could you take from the experience and apply to a challenge or opportunity you face now?

In the business world, this type of approach is used in a process called "appreciative inquiry," developed by author and researcher David Cooperrider. But it is a process that can work wonders for us in our personal and professional lives.

Consider for a moment a challenge you are having or a dilemma you'd like to resolve. Chances are, you could easily make a list of the weaknesses and mistakes on your part that led to the problem. Often, when we are trying to fix a problem or improve a situation, we focus on all that is wrong in an effort to try to correct it. This week, I'd like to challenge you to a different approach for creating what you want. Rather than focusing on everything that is wrong in a situation, pinpoint the steps that would lead to success. Failure can indeed be a learning tool, but so can success. Appreciation for the steps that have led to your best moments in life may give you the roadmap you need to get unstuck.

Success doesn't happen by accident. There are conditions, strengths, and actions that empower your success and resilience. I know that operating within my natural gifts and talents empowers me in my work. Trying to accomplish goals that lie outside of my divine purpose drains my energy. This is why, at the age of 26, I took a leap of faith to focus on building a career based on my strengths.

Perhaps in important conversations that you have, you may find that you are more effective when you take the time to think through what you need to say and even write it down. If that's what empowers you, then do it. Maybe you've noticed that you have been at your best at maintaining a healthy weight when you set short-term goals or work out with a partner. If so, set yourself up for success by creating the conditions that empower success.

There are sometimes areas in which we have not succeeded, but want to. In those instances, pinpoint the root causes of success in people who are role models for you. If you know the role model, ask them to share with you from a high point in their success. If you don't know them, pinpoint the root causes based on what you and others know.

Learning and growth often happen through the failures and adversities of life. But if you make a habit of also learning and appreciating the lessons of relationships that work, careers that soar, and lives that are meaningful, you empower yourself to overcome the inevitable obstacles you'll face on the path to success.

Christine is a woman who used the power of appreciative inquiry to build a network that transformed her business and personal life. She was a seasoned salesperson who had been the top salesperson in the company three out of the previous five years. Throughout most of her ten-year career, Christine had traveled a lot. She had lived in five cities in ten years and moved to her sixth when she decided she was simply tired of moving around. The constant change had once felt glamorous and exciting, but now it was just taking a toll on her—not just professionally, but personally. In fact, it was her personal life—or seeming lack thereof—that led her to make a change. But change did not come without trepidation. She decided to ask for a lateral move from the sales division of the company to training. She knew her prospects for raises and promotions would be stifled by this move, but it was worth it. "How much money do I really need to be happy?" she asked herself. For years, she'd measured her worth and success by her ability to increase her paycheck. With each new account she landed and subsequent bonuses and promotions, she would experience a high that only seemed to last for a couple of weeks. Then it was back to the grindstone to do it all over again.

Through honesty and self-coaching, Christine made a decision to make an intentional shift in her career. This shift allowed her to have a balance of professional gratification and personal happiness. Through this process, she figured out that her ultimate goal was to launch her own business. She had been terrific at sales. That meant that if she could figure out what enabled her to be at her best during those pivotal sales that led her to be number one in the company, she could teach those same techniques to other sales people and give them the tools to be their best. She could take those same lessons and eventually apply them to a company of her own. Here's what Christine's personal appreciative inquiry looked like:

> Think of a time when you were at your best as a salesperson. What strengths empowered you to be at your best?
>
> *Christine:* In my seventh year, it was like I was on fire. Nothing could stop me. I had momentum. That momentum was the result of several years of consistently working toward my goal of being number one. Every day when I went to work, I knew what my goal was. I watched what the most successful sales people did—they aimed for the highest dollar account opportunities, then strategically and persistently found ways to develop a relationship with the decision-makers for those accounts. They took opportunities to really understand the problem those decision-makers were having and to position themselves as a solution. It wasn't even a hard sell. It was a service sell. "What can I do for you?" was the attitude. They were patient and consistent, and eventually they had the opportunity to ask for the sale. And when they did, they asked *big*. They were bold. I followed suit. I made a decision to persevere for the long haul. I made a decision not to switch companies. I focused on my goal and went after it with all my energy!

I think that's one of my strengths. I have lots of energy and I definitely used a lot of energy to get where I am. I was excited about the future that was unfolding. I woke up every day knowing that my actions could lead me to that goal. It may sound silly, but I kept my goal in front of me— it was taped on the inside of my medicine cabinet so that when I opened the cabinet to get my toothbrush in the mornings, I would see it. And before I went to bed at night, I would also be reminded of it. I typed my goal as a one-sentence statement and printed it. Then I cut it out and placed it in my wallet, inside my desk drawer in my office, and in the corner of the windshield on the driver's side of my car. These were personal places where I usually would be the only person to see it, but they were places where I would see my goal every day throughout my day. Even though I didn't always read it, it was there and I think subconsciously, it influenced my actions and always made me look towards the future, which was bright. When I finally reached it, I felt so satisfied that I had really given it my all and made it to the finish line. Once I did it once, it became easier to keep succeeding. I think success really is just a habit.

What signature strengths do you see in Christine's descriptive answer to this appreciative inquiry? I see perseverance and patience— a willingness to make a decision to succeed and stick to it. I also see zest and enthusiasm, which likely empowered her to persevere. I also see a great deal of optimism and future-mindedness. Christine set a goal and envisioned it for herself. She stayed focused on where she was going. Now, here is a second powerful question for Christine. Take a look at how she answered this one and see what lessons you can glean.

What conditions, people, or resources were present that empowered you to be at your best when reaching your goal?

Christine: I would have to say that a turning point for me was when I got involved in a sales coaching group that was focused on goals! It was a group of salespeople from my industry who were all motivated and accomplished. We were not competing with each other; we were simply holding each other accountable, talking through obstacles, and learning from each other. We met once a week, stated our goals and what we were going to do for the week, then met up the next week to talk about our progress. For me, this was very motivating because I never wanted to come back the next week with a bunch of excuses about why I had not accomplished what I stated I would accomplish the previous week. It might sound like I was just motivated because I didn't want to be embarrassed, which doesn't sound very positive, does it? And it's true, I didn't want to be embarrassed, but the bigger issue was really about lighting a fire under me to overcome my fear of rejection.

I really believed I could be the top salesperson and I used the power of connecting with other people to pull me forward. The other salespeople in the group had many of the same fears I did and seeing that they moved forward inspired me to do the same. So I think one of the conditions that empowers me to be at my best is having like-minded people around me who are moving in the same direction. I'm also empowered by having some public accountability—telling people what I am going to do and then needing to come back and talk about it in an encouraging environment. That made it fun. The other condition was the quest to stretch myself and accomplish something I'd never accomplished before. I think that is part of why I am ready for a new challenge. I've reached my goal. It's time for some new goals—some personal goals.

These are just a couple of the conditions Christine identified. Can you see how she might be able to take the knowledge of what empowered her previously and use it to reach a goal in a totally different area of her life? You can do the same thing in your own life to create success in new areas. Become an expert at what makes you soar. It's not happenstance. You have innate strengths and abilities. There are certain conditions, people, and resources that empower you to be at your best. Do you know what they are? If you are going to succeed at higher levels and in new areas of life, it is imperative that you know who you are at your best. Start by intentionally reflecting through self-coaching.

Let's try this exercise now—a little personal appreciative inquiry. Even if the examples you can think of are small, I want you to acknowledge and appreciate your past successes. I want you to see what's already in you. Right now, you have the strength within you to grow into the kind of woman who can accomplish all that is in your heart. Let your past successes, no matter how small, ignite the confidence, hope, and creativity that will also ignite future successes.

Use your journal to repeat this personal appreciative inquiry process in the five key areas of your life. And don't just do this one time because you are reading this book. Appreciative inquiry is a skill. Choose to hone this skill as a strategic approach to success. Christine was right when she said success is a habit. Learning to raise your awareness about your strengths by noticing how you use them and the conditions under which they flourish is a powerful success "secret."

Career

Think of a time in your work when you were particularly productive, navigated a challenge effectively, or reached an important goal. Write a description of that instance here.

_____

_____

_____

_____

_____

What was the most significant character trait or strength you called on that enabled you to be at your best?

_____

_____

What are some of the other innate strengths or skills that you used? How did you use them specifically?

What conditions, people, or resources were present that empowered you to succeed in this instance? For example, perhaps you had the autonomy to make a quick decision or you collaborated with someone else to come up with a solution or you had plenty of rest the night before so you were not cranky. Imagine yourself back in the moment in time when the situation occurred and call to mind all of the circumstances that contributed to your triumph.

Look again at your answers from the previous questions. As you proceed towards your vision and goals for the future, what could you replicate from this past instance of success?

_____

_____

_____

_____

_____

Relationships

Think of a time when you were at your best in an important relationship, and as a result, that relationship thrived. Choose a specific
example of something that happened that exemplifies that. Write a
description of that instance here.

_____

_____

_____

_____

What was the most significant character trait or strength you called on
that enabled you to be at your best?

_____

_____

_____

_____

What are some of the other innate strengths or skills that you used?
How did you use them specifically?

_____

What conditions, people, or resources were present that empowered the relationship to be at its best? Perhaps it was something about the person you were in a relationship with (this will tell you something about the types of people you want to be in relationship with in the future). Maybe it was the fact that you were relaxed or not under pressure at work. Identify what it was for you in this instance.

Look again at your answers from the previous questions. As you proceed towards your vision and relationship goals for the future, what could you replicate from this past instance of success?

Finances

Think of a time when you were at your best with your money. Perhaps

it was a time when you resisted the urge to overspend or you saved consistently or you negotiated in a way that earned you more or saved you
a nice sum. Maybe it was a time when money seemed to flow to you
easily. Write a description of that instance here.

_____

_____

_____

_____

_____

What was the most significant character trait or strength you called on
that enabled you to be at your best from a financial standpoint?

_____

_____

_____

_____

What are some of the other innate strengths or skills that you used?
How did you use them specifically?

_____

_____

_____

_____

What conditions, people, or resources were present that empowered
you to be at your financial best? For example, perhaps you made a

decision not to go to the mall unless you had a specific shopping list of items you *needed* (not just wanted). Maybe your confidence was particularly high for some reason and it caused you to be bold in asking for what you wanted. Write your answer here.

_____

_____

_____

_____

_____

Look again at your answers from the previous questions. As you proceed towards your vision and financial goals for the future, what could you replicate from this past instance of success?

_____

_____

_____

_____

_____

Physical Health and Environments

Think of a time when you were at your best when it comes to your health or your physical environments (home or work environment). Perhaps you were on track with working out three or four times a week or eating healthfully. Maybe your home was clutter-free and nurturing, causing you to feel inspired.

_____

_____

_____

What was the most significant character trait or strength you called on that enabled you to be at your best physically or environmentally?

What are some of the other innate strengths or skills that you used? How did you use them specifically?

What conditions, people, or resources were present that empowered you to be at your best? For example, perhaps you had more time because your schedule was less hectic. Maybe you had someone to help you, whether a loved one or hired help. Write your answer here.

Look again at your answers from the previous questions. As you proceed towards your vision and health goals for the future, what could you replicate from this past instance of success?

Spiritual

Think of a time when you were at your best spiritually. Perhaps you heard from God very clearly. Maybe it was peace you felt in the midst of a challenge. Or perhaps you just felt particularly connected, which enabled you to love and serve others and feel like you were living on purpose. Write a description of that instance here.

What was the most significant character trait or strength you called on that enabled you to be at your best spiritually?

_____

_____

_____

_____

What are some of the other innate strengths or skills that you used? How did you use them specifically?

_____

_____

_____

_____

What conditions, people, or resources were present that empowered you to be at your spiritual best? For example, perhaps you were attending a church where you felt you were learning and connecting with like-minded people. Maybe you were spending more time around someone whose spiritual life inspired you. Perhaps you meditated first thing in the morning. Identify the conditions and write your answer here.

_____

_____

_____

_____

Look again at your answers from the previous questions. As you proceed toward your vision and spiritual goals for the future, what could you replicate from this past instance of success?

_____

Congratulations on persevering through that process! If you answered
these questions with insight and honesty, I know you will reap rewards
from it as you move forward. Success is a process, and women who
know that are always noticing what works for them when they succeed.
Just as importantly, they are able to exercise self-control (something we
will examine in-depth in the next chapter!) to replicate what works for
them. The reason it is so crucial to answer these questions using real life
instances of being at your best is that your strengths are unique to you.
It is important to glean lessons from the lives of others. Often, our best
aha! moments come from observing others. However, it can be easy to
simply try to replicate what works for someone else without acknowledging that the other person was tapping into an innate strength that
may not mirror our own. It is when you ask, "When am I at my best?"
that you dig deeper for your own personally tailored, strengths-based
plan of action.

WHAT ARE YOUR STRENGTHS?

Your strengths are traits you own, celebrate, and frequently use. They
are innate and you are energized by using them. Not only are you energized, but others feel elevated when they experience you using your
strengths. Have you ever watched a remarkable performance and felt
inspired? You were elevated as you watched strengths in action. Ever
had a teacher whose creativity allowed him or her to explain a lesson in
a way that led to your *aha!* moment? Again, you were elevated by the
use of someone else's strengths. You were better for it.

Among the many tools I have used with clients in coach training
programs and corporate training sessions is the Values in Action (VIA)

Character Strengths Survey. This measures 24 character strengths. Rather than focusing on what you "do" best, it is an assessment of who you are at your core. The test examines the gifts you possess that emerge naturally as you engage in challenges and opportunities in your life. It is free and you can take it online today.

Led by Dr. Christopher Peterson at the University of Michigan, the VIA's list of twenty-four character strengths are strengths that are universally valued across all world cultures. At the end of this list, you'll find instructions to go online and discover your top five signature strengths. The assessment is free and will take about 45 minutes to complete. For now, take a look at this list. Which five resonate most with you?

- appreciation of beauty and excellence
- bravery and valor
- capacity to love and be loved
- caution, prudence, and discretion
- citizenship, teamwork, and loyalty
- creativity, ingenuity, and originality
- curiosity and interest in the world
- fairness, equity, and justice
- forgiveness and mercy
- gratitude
- honesty, authenticity, and genuineness
- hope, optimism, and future-mindedness
- humor and playfulness
- industry, diligence, and perseverance
- judgment, critical thinking, and open-mindedness
- kindness and generosity
- leadership
- love of learning
- modesty and humility

- perspective (wisdom)
- self-control and self-regulation
- social intelligence
- spirituality, sense of purpose, and faith
- zest, enthusiasm, and energy

To find out which ones really are your signature strengths, check out the assessment on the University of Pennsylvania positive psychology website, www.authentichappiness.com. It is free, but you will have to register on the website.

TAKE A 360-DEGREE LOOK

So far, when it comes to your strengths, we've talked about the strengths you see in yourself. But the truth is that you probably have a blind spot. Strengths often come so naturally that you don't even realize their significance or how often you use them. This is why it is important to enlist the help of others to get a better assessment of your strengths. After all, it is often others who benefit most from the use of your strengths. Remember, your mission and purpose in life—while it may be enjoyable and fulfilling for you—is all about making a difference for others. The true impact of your strengths is often experienced by others in ways that are deeply profound.

When I conduct resilience workshops, I often do an exercise called a "positive introduction." It immediately breaks the ice and helps participants connect quickly, deeply, and heart-to-heart. In a small group of three or four people, each person is asked to share a pivotal moment in which they had to dig deep to unearth courage, creativity, or strength to conquer a challenge. They are then asked to explain how they became better as a result of the experience. Each person is given just a few minutes to share. Later, I ask for the group mates to reflect back on each person who shared, listing what strengths they observed from the positive introduction. The experience of hearing others acknowledge their strengths is often quite profound for the recipient of such praise.

During one session, after listening in on a participant's positive introduction, I asked her to come forward and share her pivotal moment with the group. We'll call her Jennifer. Succinctly and quickly, Jennifer described her passion for helping people find hope in the face of setbacks and disappointments. Her passion was born of pain. Her own sister committed suicide and from that experience, she came to understand the destructive power of despair and the life-giving power of God's hope. As she stood in front of the audience, they began calling out strengths they saw in her through the 60-second story she shared about her passion. "Compassion!" one woman yelled from across the room. "Courage!" another yelled. "Optimism!" another said. "I see such a loving woman standing before us," another acknowledged. "Perseverance through trials!" another said.

As Jennifer stood there, tears began to stream down her face. "I never saw all of those things," she admitted, referring to the character traits near strangers saw after just a minute of listening to a story about her at her best. "It just feels good to be acknowledged like this. I never saw all of those things about me. I was just doing what I felt led to do."

The same likely holds true for you. You have tapped into your strengths at pivotal moments in your life and you tap into them in the mundane moments too. You might not always see it, though, so I suggest you rely on people who have spent the most time with you—either now or in the past. Ask them about a time when they observed you at your best. What traits did they see in you that they think contributed to your success, no matter how small? The idea here is to truly listen to the perspective of others. Receiving acknowledgement and confirmation about strengths you may have discounted and not honored in yourself can give you the courage and boldness to move forward to a new level.

Such was the case when I made the decision to write my first book. It was not my first attempt at writing. In fact, I had attempted writing a book two previous times, but without success. The first time, I simply ran out of words. I was 22 years old and God had given me a glimpse of my future: that I would write books. But I didn't know what kind of books—or, most importantly, the *purpose* of the books I was destined to write. Without purpose, my writing didn't flow easily. Without more life experience, I simply didn't have enough to share.

Four years later, I was ready to write even though my confidence wasn't quite what I needed to get started. It was then that I had an epiphany about my life's purpose: inspiring women to live fulfilling lives, and doing so through writing and speaking. I shared my purpose with my friends and family. They were not only excited for me, but their sheer belief in my ability to do it was profound. I listened humbly, yet I treasured every bit of acknowledgment they gave me about the strengths and abilities they saw. Their ability to see me as an author and speaker impacting multitudes of people helped me believe more strongly in the possibility that I could do it. They championed my vision and asked how they could help. They saw it, and therefore, I saw it more clearly. Because I could see the invisible, I had enough faith to take a leap and pursue my dream. Hebrews 11:1 says, "Faith is the substance of things hoped for; the evidence of things not seen" (NKJV). When you begin to see your strengths, you give yourself permission to hope for bigger possibilities.

How about you? Who are your champions? Who are the people who can see your strengths clearly and reflect them back to you? Keep them around and listen to them! Their belief in you can be leverage to climb mountains, conquer challenges, and seize opportunities.

Taking a 360-degree look at yourself isn't a new idea. Leaders who truly want to improve their leadership style and that of their employees often have independent consultants come in and conduct 360-degree assessments. Rather than just getting the feedback of a boss, they solicit feedback from the boss, the boss's boss, employees, other colleagues and peers, customers, and others who come in contact with him or her. Getting an assessment from every angle gives you a clearer picture of how you are doing. Use this same approach as you assess your strengths.

SHOULD YOU IGNORE YOUR WEAKNESSES?

Acknowledging and leveraging your strengths does not necessarily mean you should pretend your weaknesses don't exist. Quite the contrary. It is actually your awareness that your weaknesses exist that helps you determine how best to use your strengths. In other words, you should directly engage your strengths to overcome your weaknesses. Studies show, for example, that helping students build on their strengths yields tremendous improvements in their grades. Helping them overcome weaknesses also yields improvements, just not nearly as drastic. The most destructive approach is to do neither. Students who are not given any feedback show virtually no improvements over time, and often decline in their academic performance. Likewise, workers who feel ignored by their employer are at the greatest risk for becoming disengaged from their jobs. The bottom line: focusing on weaknesses is a much less effective tool than focusing on strengths, but ignoring your performance and opportunities for growth altogether is destructive.

This bit of knowledge is powerful for your own personal growth, but also for developing a leadership style—whether at work, in your community, or with your children—that empowers those you lead.

WHAT ARE YOUR WEAKNESSES?

You should not ignore your weaknesses. We've established that. But what exactly are they? If you are like many women, you can easily ramble off a list of all the abilities and talents you feel you lack. But acknowledging your weaknesses isn't about beating yourself up. It is not about obsessing over all the things that are wrong with you, but instead about building on what's right. And there is plenty right about you.

What are some areas in which you consistently struggle? Even when you try hard, you seem to backslide or become frustrated. What seems easy for others sometimes feels insurmountable for you. List them here.

_____

_____

_____

_____

_____

USE YOUR STRENGTHS TO COMPEN-SATE FOR YOUR WEAKNESSES

The point of raising your awareness about the places where you are weak is to prevent those weaknesses from sabotaging your success. Don't be afraid to admit them. The truth is powerful when you use that knowledge to move you forward. Consider your signature strengths as well as some of the strengths you identified when you asked the question, "When am I at my best?" Now take a look at the list you wrote above. Which weakness most threatens to sabotage your success?

_____

_____

_____

_____

_____

Ponder this: How could you tap one of your strengths to address that weakness?

_____

_____

_____

_____

Learning to use your strengths to solve challenges, especially the challenge of overcoming weaknesses, is a critical success skill.

CAN YOUR STRENGTHS EVER BECOME WEAKNESSES?

Consider Robin. A sharp, hardworking woman in her mid-thirties,

Robin has been steadily climbing the corporate ladder at work while raising a family with her husband. People often marvel at Robin's Superwoman-like abilities. *How do you do it?* she is often asked. It's a flattering question, but the truth is that Robin's success is on the brink of crumbling in more ways than one. In fact, her employer has given her a stern warning and assigned her an internal executive coach to help her deal with the fact that none of the people who work for her seem to stay at the company very long. And the ones who hold on are all applying for positions in other departments. They are stressed. One employee who thrived in another department for several years seems to be completely disengaged from his work. At home, Robin and her husband cannot seem to get through one evening without snapping at each other. But lately, Mike has quit snapping back. He seems not to care very much about what she says anymore. "It's like he's tolerating me," Robin says. "He's not angry. He's not nice. He's just lukewarm."

Robin, by most people's standards, has been on the fast track to professional success. She is a marketing director in a major company. Her income is impressive, especially given her age. And she has a list of awards and accolades that validate her competence. In fact, one of the things she is most known for is not just taking charge of a project or situation, but getting to the bottom of any issues or challenges that may need to be addressed in order to successfully move the project forward.

Robin is never afraid to confront problems—or people. It comes naturally to her and it has worked to her advantage as she climbed her way to director more quickly than most. However, her strength of "taking command" sometimes rubs people the wrong way. She is opinionated and often not collaborative. When managing people, she explains, she is simply addressing the obvious. It doesn't occur to her that not everyone is as comfortable confronting and discussing problems as she is. When people on her team at work don't line up with her ideas, she has a hard time slowing down and considering their insights before charging ahead with plans. As a result, her team members stopped sharing their ideas. They see her as demanding and controlling—and at times, intimidating.

Unfortunately her husband, Mike, has begun to see her that way too. Early in their marriage it worked fine. He was in graduate school and working full-time, so he appreciated the way she took charge with the kids. But now that he has more time on his hands and he is spending more time with the children, childrearing has become a source of tension. It seems like nothing he does is quite right. From Mike's perspective, he is constantly being told what to do and how to do it. Frankly, he's tired of it. "Why are we arguing over how I comb the girls' hair?" Mike wonders. "Most women are complaining that they have to do all the work. My wife is complaining that I don't comb hair like she does. It seems like nothing I do is good enough. I'm tired of the criticism. If she wants to do it all, at this point I'm so exasperated, I might just let her."

Robin is experiencing what is called a "shadow side" to her strengths. It is when a strength that works to your advantage gets overused to the point that it becomes a weakness. Her ability to take charge is a fantastic strength that catapulted her career forward and worked well for her family when her husband was working and going to school simultaneously. But now that she is managing more people and her husband is available to help too, her strength is sabotaging her marriage and any chances for further advancement at work. What should she do?

Robin should use self-awareness to notice the powerful impact she has on people when she operates in her strength and be intentional about ensuring that that impact aligns with her goals. If her goal is a happy marriage, then being opinionated about things that don't matter is counterproductive. Remember, successful women *think* differently. They are able to notice when their own behaviors lead them away from success rather than toward it. And they are flexible enough to make changes and adjustments to get what they really want.

Robin was asked, "How can you tap into your faith to balance out your tendency to be overly commanding in your relationship with Mike?" Here was her response:

> When I really think about it, it was hard doing so much
> alone when Mike was in school and working. I felt like
> a single parent most days because I was handling all the

parenting stuff alone. Even though I didn't admit it, I think I became somewhat resentful of that. I'm glad that's not the situation we are in any more. I am grateful that he wants to share the responsibility and I need to let him do that in his own way, without me telling him exactly how I want it done. I need to appreciate what a blessing he really is. The things we are arguing over are just not worth it.

On the VIA Character Strengths Survey, Robin's top strength is gratitude. Tapping into her natural propensity toward that strength, Robin shifted her perspective about how to engage with her husband. She used that same strength of gratitude to re-engage her employees. Acknowledging their efforts publicly and expressing her thanks through rewards and recognition, she slowly but surely began to undo some of the damage she'd done. Her approach worked. Two years later, she was promoted to vice president. Even better, she and Mike grew closer than ever.

HIRE FOR STRENGTHS

Remember Cookie Lee? The marketing-executive-turned-jewelry-designer launched a company in her quest to have a career and be at home with her kids. One of her top strengths is enthusiasm. But she has also made it a habit to tap into the strengths of others by finding their passion and having them work from that place. "I surround myself with people who know the answers. I don't have to be strong at everything. I find staff to work in the area where they are passionate." This attitude taps into another foundational principle for your success: Leverage your strengths and the strengths of others.

Successful women don't ignore the obvious. They know where they are weak and they look for ways to shore up those weaknesses by finding others whose strengths they can tap into. When possible, they hire out weaknesses so that they can spend their time focused on the areas in which they excel. How might this apply to you right now? For example, if success has eluded you when it comes to exercising and eating right, connect with those who can help. If you have the financial resources, this might mean hiring a personal trainer, signing up for tennis or kick-boxing classes, or ordering healthy meals rather than fast food when you go out for dinner. But even these options, if you are creative, don't have to cost a lot. Be resourceful when shoring up your weaknesses. How could you use your strengths to benefit someone who has what you need? Barter and exchange if you need to. Refuse to make excuses.

Just as it is important to "hire" strengths, it is also important to be willing to fire for strengths. As you move to higher levels and step into new territory, having the right people around you is essential. Pay attention to others' strengths and weaknesses. Don't rely on people to accomplish tasks that they are not uniquely equipped to accomplish. You will only set yourself up for failure and set them up for frustration. Refuse to allow fear to cause you to keep people in positions and places that do not allow them to use their strengths. The most successful women are experts not only at tapping into their own strengths, but the strengths of others.

Your strengths are literally what make you stronger. Using your strengths, you get results faster and with seemingly less effort. Tapping into your strengths is a form of leverage. You can do more with less. As you move toward all that is calling you forward, focus on that which makes you stronger—the God-given abilities that come so naturally to you. Build on them. Celebrate them. Have fun using them!

Every Woman Should Know

- Using your strengths creates authentic positive emotion for you personally while also elevating those around you.

- Stories about a pivotal moment in your life have a powerful, inspirational quality and an ability to reveal your strengths.

- When managing others, giving strengths-based feedback is more effective than focusing on weaknesses. However, ignoring them altogether is far more damaging than either option. Women who are great managers give feedback.

PERSONAL COACHING TOOLKIT: POWER QUESTIONS TO TAP INTO YOUR STRENGTHS

Answer each of these questions in a journal or with a coach or friend who can listen objectively and give you the space to explore your answers without attempting to give you the answers.

1. Consider a pivotal moment in your life when you had to dig deep to unearth courage, strength, and creativity to move forward. What innate strengths did you use to overcome the challenge?

2. Take the VIA Character Strengths assessment at www.authentichappiness.com, a free website sponsored by the University of Pennsylvania. What are your top five signature strengths?

3. Which of your signature strengths most resonates with you? Consider the goal that is nearest and dearest to your heart. How could you employ this strength to help you reach your goal?

4. In what ways do you focus too much on your weaknesses?

5. Talk to an adult who knew you when you were a girl. It can be a parent, sibling, friend, or other relative. Ask them to consider a memorable moment, such as a challenge or opportunity, in which you thrived. What strengths did they see in you at that age?

6. Talk to someone who is active in your life now—a relative, friend, or coworker, for example. What innate strengths do they see in you?

7. Consider your personal vision for your life. What obstacle most threatens to throw you off course? Which one of your innate strengths will most help you conquer the obstacle? How?

8. What weakness have you been perpetually trying to fix, to no avail? How could you shore up that weakness by tapping

into one or more of your strengths? Identify a specific action step. For example, someone who has a weakness for showing up on time and is chronically late might tap her strength for fairness by putting the shoe on the other foot, so to speak. Is she being fair to others' time and energy when she forces them to pay for her bad habits by sitting and waiting for her to show up?

9. What strengths are you lacking that you think would help you move to the next level more quickly and easily? Who do you know who possesses this strength? Sometimes, it's not about *having* a particular strength, but knowing that it would help you on your way to your goal. Be intentional about brainstorming or collaborating with those whose strengths are different from and complement your own.

10. In what way is it time to stretch outside your comfort zone? How will you use your top strength to do that?

Think Differently:

Stop focusing on your weaknesses. Start building on your strengths.

Build Your Muscle of Self-Control

———— ✳ ————

*Why your talent isn't enough and how to develop
the trait that will take you to the top*

Key Lessons:

- Discipline trumps talent when it comes to high levels of achievement
- Stretch yourself to build success muscles
- Sheer grit is your secret weapon

Imagine yourself at four years old. You're in preschool and all the other kids are outside. Your teacher offers you a deal: you can have your choice of a marshmallow, cookie, or pretzel right now—whichever you prefer. Or, if you wait for her to return to the room in 15 minutes, she'll give you *two* of your favorite treat. What does four-year-old you do? Bite into your treat as soon as she leaves the room? Or do you hold out for a double reward?

The answer to that question may predict more about a child's future than you think. The famous "Stanford marshmallow experiment" shed some light on the relationship between self-control and success. More than 600 children between the ages of four and six took part. Some children bit into the treat the moment the adult left the room, while others did their best to hold out. They sniffed the treat, covered their eyes, and found ways to distract themselves. But for many, the temptation was just too great. They ate the treat before the researcher returned. However, a third of the children who attempted to delay gratification succeeded and scored a second treat.

More than a decade passed before researchers discovered the most amazing results of the study. Teenagers who had been able to delay gratification at a young age were deemed "significantly more competent" by their parents and had higher SAT scores. The ability to delay gratification—in favor of doing homework, learning a challenging new skill, or persevering through difficult circumstances—can lead to greater success in life.*

What does this mean for you? The fourth success habit you want to develop is *self-control*. Whether you want to succeed at losing weight and maintaining it, getting out of debt and staying out, or building a business or career, self-control is essential. Without it, we blow our best plans and chances for success.

We often hear books and motivational speakers, even preachers and business leaders, tout "secrets of success." Are there really any secrets, though? I've always been skeptical. That is, until I discovered some factual research about the power of discipline in the lives of the most highly successful people in the world.

If you are one of the few who holds discipline and self-control as top signature strengths, you are rare indeed. Among Americans, these strengths fall near the bottom of the 24 universal character strengths. If there is any strength you should seek to build, though, this one would be it. Successful women know discipline is their friend. It's not exactly a sexy topic, but it's one that must be mastered if you are to succeed at the highest levels—whether in your work or relationships, health or finances. In studies and real world examples, self-control trumps talent when it comes to success. It's not IQ or SAT scores that best predict student success. It's self-discipline. Self-discipline also predicts whether students will improve over the course of a school year. The same holds true for adults. While it is difficult to find Scriptures

---

* Walter Mischel, Ebbe B. Ebbesen, and Antonette Raskoff Zeiss. "Cognitive and Attentional Mechanisms in Delay of Gratification." *Journal of Personality and Social Psychology* 21, no. 2 (1972): 204-18.

about the importance of being talented or smart or intelligent, there are plenty of Scriptures about the merits of discipline and self-control:

- For lack of discipline they will die, led astray by their own great folly. –Proverbs 5:23
- Like a city whose walls are broken through is a person who lacks self-control. –Proverbs 25:28
- But the fruit of the Spirit is love, joy, peace, patience, kindness, goodness, faithfulness, gentleness and self-control. –Galatians 5:22-23
- Make every effort to add to your faith goodness; and to goodness, knowledge; and to knowledge, self-control; and to self-control, perseverance; and to perseverance, godliness; and to godliness, mutual affection; and to mutual affection, love. –2 Peter 1:5-7

DISCIPLINE AND SELF-CONTROL: ARE THEY ONE AND THE SAME?

We often hear discipline and self-control lumped together. In Galatians 5:22, which describes the fruit of the spirit, the words "discipline" and "self-control" are used interchangeably depending on which translation of the text you read. You need both, but I want to point out a distinction. Self-control is the ability in the heat of the moment to resist temptation or embrace that which will move you in the right direction. Discipline is consistency in addition to perseverance. It is about setting a goal and sticking with it repeatedly through obstacles and setbacks, disappointments and frustrations. It is the ability to take specific action day in and day out—and it ultimately leads to the results you are hoping for. It is a series of self-controlled moments that lead you to repetitively engage in behavior that will lead you to your ultimate goal.

For example, consider my client Marlene. Marlene's goal was to make the leap from corporate America to owning her own successful business. Her job required about 45 hours of her time each week, and through coaching we identified approximately ten hours per week available to her to grow the business part-time—two nights per week for three hours each night and four hours on Saturday mornings. With her demanding schedule, it would be essential for Marlene to maximize her time during these ten hours.

She did so beautifully. First, she identified all of the potential obstacles to having focused, disciplined work time to build the business: interruptions from phone calls and e-mail, her preteen twins and her husband, demands from after-hours work from her regular job (her boss sometimes sent her texts and e-mails on her work cell phone), and the temptation to lay on the sofa at the end of the day and watch her favorite television shows. Then we addressed each one of those potential distractions in order to eliminate them. The most important step was a family meeting to talk about Marlene's goals and what they would mean to the family. She talked about her dream and what it would mean if she could launch a business—she'd get to work from home, spend more time with all of them, and during the period that she was working the business part-time, they'd enjoy some additional income to perhaps take a vacation with. This got the kids excited and on board with the goal. Her husband was already supportive.

Marlene decided to turn off the cell phone during her business work hours and not take any calls from the house phone (and whoever answered the home phone was instructed to say she was unavailable and take a message). This took discipline, but after a couple of failed work sessions in which she answered the phone and veered off track, Marlene learned the importance of sticking to this rule! Lastly, she chose to do the part-time work on evenings when her favorite television shows were not on. This way there was little temptation to go sit on the sofa rather than work. The key to Marlene's success is she didn't overdo it. But at each step of the way, she needed self-control:

- Each time she arrived home and felt tempted to do something other than her second job, especially after working eight to nine hours at her day job.

- Each time she heard the home phone ring and wondered who it was and what they were calling about.

- Each time she told herself it would be no big deal to leave the cell phone on while she worked, just in case something important came through via text or e-mail.

- Each time her mind wandered to something else she could be doing.

Each day, Marlene exercised discipline by:

- Remaining consistent in moving toward her goal of full-time business ownership.

- Trying again when she failed to exercise self-control in some way.

- Reminding herself of her vision. It pulled her forward when the business wasn't growing as quickly as she would have liked and helped her stay motivated towards the big picture.

Coach You:

What one disciplined act would lead you to one of your meaningful goals? What self-control would you have to exhibit in order to conquer the potential distractions to that goal?

Through both discipline and self-control, Marlene succeeded in her goal. It indeed took a great deal of discipline (perseverance plus consistency)—five and half years of it. At the end of that time, though, Marlene gave notice to her day job and made the leap into full-time business ownership.

BUILDING THE MUSCLE OF SELF-CONTROL

Self-control is directly tied to delayed gratification. In a culture where so much is instant, we are tempted to be impatient, to bypass hard work and effort, and to expect success quickly. In fact, a common complaint among older workers is that the youngest generation in the workplace often feels entitled to faster promotions and raises than previous generations. Could it be that the onslaught of instant gratification this generation has grown up with is a contributor to this phenomenon?

Psychologists who study procrastination point out that one of the reasons e-mail is such an easy distraction is that it provides the instant gratification of accomplishing a task. Even if the task accomplished is not a priority in the moment or even particularly purposeful, it meets a basic human tendency to be gratified by progress. Focusing on the report you have to do won't provide that quick gratification, and so you exchange the important work for more immediate gratification.

Knowing this information about the effects of gratification can equip you to create strategies and empower you to achieve big goals. First, recognize that you need a sense of gratification that is provided by accomplishment along your road to a goal. If the only cause for celebration and gratification is the finish line, you may give up long before you get there. There are a couple of reasons for this that you will find helpful to remember:

- Gratification is an element of happiness. You may recall from habit two that happiness is the one thing we pursue for its own sake. Creating a sense of instant gratification, even if you personally manufacture it, is a great way to use the pursuit of happiness to the advantage of your goals.

- Positive emotion literally and physically energizes you. A burst of gratification is like a B12 shot for your goals.

- By creating incremental goals and celebrating the achievement of them, you can get the short bursts of gratification that keep you motivated to move forward.

Let me give you an example of this. When I am writing a book, I set goals for how many words I intend to write each day that I am working on the book. I know if I succeeded on any given day by two things: how easily the words flow and whether I reach my quantitative goal. These two measures work together because if the words flow, reaching my word-count goal happens almost effortlessly. But that effortlessness happens only with a great deal of self-control.

I didn't realize this until engaging in a bit of self-coaching. I used the "When are you at your best?" model to identify the conditions that strengthened me to reach my goal. I followed up with curiosity about the conditions that caused me to be at my worst. Understanding both of these can empower you to create a uniquely designed success formula that you can repeat day after day to reach your goals. That's where discipline kicks in, but it is informed discipline—strategic by nature. By asking myself a few simple but powerful questions, I became aware of some key factors that enable discipline and self-control, including a sense of continual gratification while moving towards the ultimate daily goal.

Here's a peek into that coaching conversation on a day when I wrote easily and reached my goal followed by a day when I wrote virtually nothing. I started by asking myself what I did to enable success in reaching the goal the previous day:

> **Question:** You were at your best yesterday. What conditions were in place yesterday that made your writing go so well?
>
> **Me:** Well, I was very intentional about creating boundaries around my space and time so that I could focus 100 percent. I cleared my calendar for the day. I got up early, ate breakfast, prayed, and meditated. I specifically asked God to write through me and use me as His vessel. I also meditated on a simple idea: that I am a professional writer, that I know how to do this, and that this is my purpose. I informed those in my office that I would be unavailable the first half of the day, but would check e-mail around noon. I turned off my cell phone and cut off the Internet connection to avoid the temptation to surf the net. I headed to my office, lit a candle, and played soft music in the background. On the whiteboard in my office I drew a thermometer. At the top I marked my word-count goal and I drew marks in ten increments symbolizing progress towards the

goal. As the words flowed and my word count increased, I marked off each increment. I love the visual representation of my progress and the way it kept me focused toward a specific goal. It was gratifying each time I went to the whiteboard to mark my progress.

Question: What happened today when you didn't do so well with your writing?

Me: I was very frustrated with my lack of progress today. I can trace it back to how the morning started. I fell asleep late and got up later than the previous morning. I did not pray and meditate before I wrote. I left the phone on vibrate rather than turning it off completely, and ended up on the phone a couple of times. I also forgot to erase yesterday's progress thermometer from the whiteboard. It was midmorning before I began tracking my progress in a visual way. By then, I was frustrated because I'd written very little and spent time responding to e-mails. I also scheduled lunch with a friend today and once I got back to my office, I found it hard to refocus.

In hindsight, it seems so obvious that there were multiple reasons in this scenario why the first day flowed extremely well while the second day was pretty much a disaster. Stopping to identify the specific steps taken that enabled success gave me a formula I use to this day. The formula requires a lot of self-control in the heat of the moment. But that self-control becomes easier to exercise when I set myself up for success by eliminating and minimizing the distractions that threaten my self-control. And "manufacturing" instant gratification keeps me on track to the ultimate gratification of reaching the bigger goal. The discipline of persevering consistently through the process leads to the end product—what you are reading now, the big goal. Use these same principles to reach a big goal you have. You may be motivated by different specifics, but as a human being, the principles still apply.

THE POWER OF STICKING TO IT

"The passion for stretching yourself and sticking to it, even (or especially) when it's not going well, is the hallmark of the growth mindset," Dr. Carol Dweck explains in her book *Mindset*. So what's your mindset when it comes to the most important goal in your life? Are you passionate and relentless? Do you take steps toward it every single day? Passion certainly fuels perseverance, and discipline often requires that stick-to-it spirit. For a fortunate few, discipline and self-control come more naturally. In fact, it can be a signature strength. But for most of us, it requires a serious commitment of effort.

Many people for whom success is elusive brush off their failure by insisting that successful people never feel fear, are immensely talented, and naturally lucky. Nothing could be further from the truth. Successful women feel fear, but through a growth mindset they learn to move forward in spite of their fears. Many successful women are quite talented, but not any more so than a whole lot of other less successful women. But they continually hone their skills. They are not afraid to shed light on areas where they could improve. They practice with great discipline the skills they need in order to move forward. They make decisions and stick with them through faith and perseverance. They encounter luck, but they usually don't call it that. They know that when opportunity strikes, the only way to be lucky is to be prepared. And preparation takes discipline.

The key to developing self-control is to remember that it is like a muscle. You build it up over time. When you first begin exercising it, it won't feel fun. It will hurt. You won't feel like doing it again the next day because your muscles are sore.

Since self-control is like a muscle, you must remember that it is a very limited resource and it can become fatigued. When practiced in challenging (but not overwhelming) doses, the muscle becomes strengthened.

GOAL SETTING

"We could not be happy without setting ourselves goals," says economist Richard Layard in his book *Happiness: Lessons from a New Science.* "Prod any happy person and you will find a project."

This is a wonderful revelation. It goes back to what we discussed early in the book: Success is a harmony of service, happiness, and achievement. Goal setting falls in the achievement category. Happily successful women set inspired goals and move toward them. They intuitively set goals that tap into their strengths, curiosity, and purpose. They know that the best kinds of goals are divinely inspired. Those are the goals they were meant to accomplish; the goals that will teach them the most and develop them fully into the women they were meant to be; and the goals that will flow most easily because they will be helped along by God Himself, who often orchestrates opportunities and connections they alone simply could not. Happily successful women don't set goals, write them down, and then stuff them in a drawer. They get busy taking action that will bring the goals to pass.

If you have ever known that depressed feeling of being stuck without a clear vision for where you are going, you've experienced the boost in energy that comes when you engage in a meaningful new project. It is summed up best in Proverbs 29:18: "Where there is no vision, the people perish" (KJV). In other words, they *die.* Inspired goals, and the achievement of them, give you life.

You'll know an inspired goal by whether you feel led by it rather than dragged by it. When you are led, you move forward naturally. Even if you procrastinate on it, you can't let it go. When you don't move towards it, you are frustrated with yourself. If the goal isn't inspired, it feels like a burden. You would be relieved to let it go. It doesn't tap into your strengths or fulfill your purpose. It may be impressive. It may be what someone else wants you to do, but it's not truly yours. It's a goal, just not the right goal for you.

STRETCH BEYOND
YOUR COMFORT ZONE

Some goals we shy away from because they feel too hard. You can convince yourself that you don't have what it takes, and therefore there's no use attempting it. Sometimes that's true. There are some goals for which we have no talent whatsoever or not *enough* talent to go after it. For example, I'm not a particularly technical person. There may be lots of great opportunities in the field of information technology, but there's no use in attempting that career path. I would hate it. And frankly, I'd be really bad at it. It's not my passion or purpose. So to be clear, some goals feel too hard and you shouldn't bother with them because they fall outside of your purpose. You have no passion for it. Without purpose or passion, it is difficult to persevere.

I have several goals, but one in particular feels like a real stretch. I've always been in awe of distance runners. Even while on the track team in high school, I hated doing the one-mile warm-up. And when my knee started bothering me in college, I gave up running altogether—and I wasn't the least bit sad about it. But in 2009, I began running for the first time in years. I couldn't believe it! It became my solace—a place to clear my mind and stretch beyond my comfort zone. It also became a metaphor for my life. The more I ran, the more confident I became in my ability to stretch myself and do other things that required discipline. Now there's an idea rolling around in my mind that I cannot seem to escape: Running a half-marathon this year. So, I'm going to go for it! I've begun training for the 13.1-mile run. This week, I'm creating a vision board to keep me inspired and excited about all of my goals for the year, especially this one.

NINE WAYS TO STICK WITH YOUR GOALS

What about you? What goal would stretch you beyond your comfort zone? Is it time to stretch beyond your comfort zone? Whether your goal is to change careers, eliminate drama from your life, pay off your debt, or run a half-marathon, use these strategies to stretch yourself.

- *Pick one, just one.* Rather than making a laundry list of goals and attempting to reach them all at once, choose one to focus on at a time. What's your most important goal

this year? Get a laser focus on it. It takes energy to reach
a goal, so harness your energy on the one that matters
most. Choose a goal that intrigues you—one that you find
inspiring and meaningful. You don't have to know exactly
how you'll get there right now. You just need to know that
you are willing to commit to taking the steps to get there.

- *Make a decision to pursue it.* It's easy to talk about something you want to do. But something shifts in you when
  you make a decision to go after it. Stop saying, "I sure wish
  I could" and start saying, "I'm going to!" Make a decision.
  A decision indicates your belief that it is possible. Once a
  decision is made, action must follow.

- *Pinpoint your inspiration.* People who succeed at reaching
  their goals use the power of inspiration to get there. When
  you are inspired, your motivation comes from within. You
  see the purpose behind your goal and that purpose fuels
  perseverance and passion. Want to lose that 20 pounds?
  Ask yourself why. What will it give you to lose those 20
  pounds? Why is it worth the effort?

- *Find a motivated partner.* There is power in numbers.
  Working with someone else who is moving in the same
  direction is a powerful experience. Who else is motivated
  to accomplish a similar goal? Is there an organization or
  group you could join to hold you accountable? If not,
  could you start one informally? Be proactive about part-
  nering with others. Not only does it give you accountability, but you learn from one another, encourage one another,
  and celebrate together.

- *Reach out for support.* You don't need to reinvent the wheel
  to accomplish your goal. There is someone out there who
  has done this before—or knows someone who has. And
  if there isn't anyone you know, I bet there's a book on it.
  When I set out to write my first book in 1999, I'd never

done it before. I bought a book about how to write and publish your book, and I followed it! Four months later, *Rich Minds, Rich Rewards* was published.

- *Create a vision board.* Keep your goal in front of you. "When you can see the invisible, you can do the impossible," T.D. Jakes once said. Create a visually inspiring spot that reminds you of where you are headed and what it will feel like to reach that goal. Look at it often. Imagine yourself blasting through obstacles and reaching your destination.

- *Expect a challenge and determine to keep pressing forward.* Be ready for some obstacles. You might sometimes take three steps forward and two steps back. That's part of the process. When you stumble, don't give up—*get up*!

- *Plan for the obstacles upfront.* Researchers in the area of goal setting say it is essential to remember that reaching a goal is as much about the process as the destination. And sometimes the process is more of a zig-zag than a straight line. Remember that there is often more to learn from failure than success, so when your journey to the goal line meets a hurdle, don't stop. Jump! Keep pressing on. The finish line lies just ahead.

- *Reward and recharge after each milestone.* Research also shows that our energy can become depleted after exerting a great deal of effort towards a goal. Giving yourself time to refuel before charging ahead is sometimes the smartest move you can make. Think of your journey like a long road trip. If you drive indefinitely without an oil change or refueling, you'll burn out and run out of fuel. As you reach milestones along your journey, give yourself a break. Celebrate with rewards. You'll get to your destination soon enough, so enjoy the journey.

Every Woman Should Know

- "Grit" among young children is a better predictor of later success in life than IQ scores.

- When NASA chooses astronauts, they seek out people who don't have simply a track record of success, but who have had significant failures and bounced back.

- Celebrating effort over talent or ability is a key to motivating and inspiring success.

PERSONAL COACHING TOOLKIT: POWER QUESTIONS TO DISCIPLINE YOURSELF

1. In what ways have you embraced a fixed mindset, believing your abilities are set in stone and cannot be improved?

2. Which ability would be most transformative for you to be able to improve? How would it change your life to gain that ability?

3. What would be a first step towards enhancing that ability? What people or other resources could help you?

4. Think of a goal you have wanted to reach for some time. In the heat of the moment, when you need to perform a particular task that moves you toward that goal, what is your biggest temptation or distraction?

5. What could you do to eliminate or minimize that temptation or distraction? Who or what would almost guarantee you success in eliminating or minimizing that distraction?

6. What ability that you currently do not have would give you new confidence to reach the inspired vision you've set for yourself?

7. If you could have a conversation with God in this moment,

in what way do you think He would say He wanted you to adopt a growth mindset? In other words, where have you simply settled and decided that something in your life is impossible?

8. In what way do you most lack discipline (consistency plus perseverance)? In what way do you most lack self-control (the ability in the heat of the moment to take a specific action in the right direction)?

9. What are you willing to do about your lack of discipline in that area? What are you willing to do about your lack of self-control in that area?

10. What action could you take today to move in the direction of greater discipline and self-control?

Think Differently:

Make a decision to practice the skill of discipline until you master it. Refuse to ever again say, "I don't have any discipline." Speak life into your dreams by saying only that which will reinforce your goal of developing more discipline and self-control in your life.

Cultivate Positive Emotion

———※———

*How a surprising but easy formula will save
your relationships and transform your life*

Key Lessons

- Happiness leads to success—not the other way around
- Build an emotional bank account of positive experiences
- Don't make the big decisions when you're in an emotional rut

A famous study of nuns exemplifies the power of positive emotion in the most profound way. Researchers analyzed the journals of 180 nuns who had entered a convent in 1930, when they were between the ages of 18 and 32. The number of positive emotional words and sentences the nuns used in their journals was tracked, as well as their longevity.

The results were stunning. The nuns who expressed the most positive emotion in their writing—those in the top 25 percent for positive emotion—lived on average 9.4 years longer than the nuns in the bottom 25 percent who expressed the least amount of positive emotion! Positive emotion, as described in their early-life autobiographies, was a predictor of longevity 60 years later. What is particularly remarkable about this study is that the nuns' lifestyles were so similar that there are few to no variables to account for this discrepancy. Think about it. None of them were married. None had children. They shared a similar diet. Their professions were the same and they all lived in the same place. What can we learn from this? Positive emotion is a powerful ally.

Happily successful women have a secret: they see fun as an essential element of success. As a result, they have discovered an important truth. Happiness doesn't come from success. In fact, it's the other way around: *Success comes from happiness.* Through interviews and coaching sessions with hundreds of women over the years and as a happily successful woman, it is clear to me that when a woman is both passionate and content with her life and her work, she is the epitome of success. Amazingly, research confirms this as fact. Happiness actually *causes* success. For years, it was argued that successful people are happier because they've achieved what they wanted. This belief asserts that your happiness is dependent upon success. This is the very reason why so many women and men alike chase after possessions and people and accolades. They mistakenly believe that if only they had X, they would finally be happy. "If I get that promotion," "If I finally get married," "If I get my dream home," "If I make my business successful…then I'll really be happy."

No matter how you define success, the truth is that happiness comes in the journey. The positive emotion and moments that are created along the way actually make you emotionally, physically, and mentally stronger, thereby enabling you to make wiser decisions, forge stronger relationships, and better handle the unexpected turns and challenges of life. *This* empowers you to be successful.

Research now shows that the positive emotion associated with happiness actually equips people to handle adversity better, bounce back from setbacks, see the big picture, and live longer. Eccelsiastes 3:12-13 teaches us that "there is nothing better for people than to be happy and to do good while they live. That each of them may eat and drink, and find satisfaction in all their toil—this is the gift of God." Likewise, Nehemiah 8:10 reminds us that "the joy of the LORD is your strength."

Both of these Scriptures have actually been proven through scientific research. Dr. Barbara Frederickson, an award-winning researcher at the University of North Carolina, has conducted groundbreaking studies on the power of positive emotion and its role in boosting happiness and performance. I want to share a few highlights of this research with you that will be relevant in your success journey. Let's begin not with a discussion of the positive, but the negative.

POWER OF NEGATIVE EMOTION

Negative emotion is more psychologically powerful than positive. When you have a negative experience, it takes more than just one equally positive experience to bounce back. Negative emotion causes powerful physiological changes in the body and mind. Reversing those changes requires more than an equal dose of positive emotion. In fact, it takes about three positive experiences to balance the effects of one negative experience.

What does this mean for you in a practical sense? If you are giving feedback to an employee, for example, and the feedback is negative, you could balance your delivery of that feedback by maintaining a light tone of voice, acknowledging several positive decisions she's made or actions she's taken (such as a signature strength she used during a recent project), and nodding and listening as she asks questions rather than cutting her short. All of these positives will make the one negative an easier pill to swallow.

The three to one positive to negative emotion ratio is particularly important in relationships. Studies have consistently shown that when the ratio of positive to negative falls below that number, a relationship begins to break down. Listening and collaborating becomes more challenging.

Teams in particular can become gridlocked and much less productive when the ratio falls below three positives to one negative. Think about a team you worked on in which there was too much criticism and negativity. Now picture that team in a meeting. Some team members have crossed arms. Others attempt to make contributions but feel that they're not being heard. Other team members disengage altogether and sit passively in the meeting, murmuring under their breath or rolling their eyes at the members in leadership positions. Too much negativity in the workplace is detrimental to productivity. It undermines trust and loyalty.

This three-to-one ratio must be even higher in a marriage relationship. In a marriage, says researcher Dr. John Gottman, the positive to negative emotion ratio must be at five to one to maintain a healthy relationship and avoid divorce. Cultivating positive emotion is the best success strategy.

BUILDING AN EMOTIONAL BANK ACCOUNT

But negativity between people is not the only type of emotion that is detrimental to your productivity, performance, and personal well-being. Both negative and positive emotions build over time, like a bank account. Positive emotions are deposits added to your account, cushioning the blow of any negative experiences you may face. Negative emotions are debits that subtract from your account. Too many debits without deposits can leave you overdrawn and without the resources to manage the everyday stresses that come your way, let alone the major ones that occasionally show up, unwelcomed and unexpected. So it is essential to be intentional about building a bank account of positive emotional experiences.

Too many negative experiences (resulting in negative emotions) weaken your ability to deal with stress and adversity. It also skews your perspective, decreasing your ability to see clearly. Here's an example of a skewed perspective. Maybe you have had a rough week at the office and a coworker tells you your boss is out to get you. "Remember on Monday she corrected your work when it was really just fine?" the coworker says. "And on Wednesday she was against the brilliant idea you pitched during the staff meeting, and just yesterday she told you she would call your client to try to smooth things over from that event last week. She didn't even call like she said she would!"

Before your coworker pointed out all these events, you hadn't thought much about your boss's corrections on Monday. You were disappointed but not upset when she didn't jump on your idea in the staff meeting, and you figured she just got too busy to call the client yesterday. But now your wheels are turning. Suddenly, your sensitivity to her behavior is heightened. Your coworker's argument is convincing, and you begin to recall a lot of other things your boss has done recently that could be perceived as a subtle ploy to ease you out of the department. Maybe she's intimidated by you and doesn't want you around anymore.

When you come in the next week you're playing defense, no matter what your boss says or does to you. You perceive her every action as negative, whether or not it's really intended that way, and are unable to notice all the positives. The following week, after giving you negative feedback, she mentions to you that a position may open up in another department in a few months. If you can master this project she's about to give to you, she thinks you'd be great for it. She remarks that you are the leading associate in the department. There are some areas where you need to improve, and it will take a little effort on your part to make the improvements. The new job would mean a better title, but no raise—not yet anyway. It could lead to a pay increase in another year. Because of your new belief that she is "out to get you," you perceive the conversation as negative. You fail to see the compliment in her remarks and only glean the perceived negatives.

This emotional bank account builds over time, actually accumulating like a reserve. This can help explain, for example, the benefit of a positive childhood in fortifying a person for his or her adult years. If you make it out of childhood with a surplus of positive experiences in your emotional bank account, it can soften the blow of adversity and challenges in the future. Even if such is not the case for your childhood, beginning to build more positive emotion into your life can strengthen you for the future still ahead for you.

Research on positive emotions reflects much of the spiritual wisdom found throughout Scripture:

- The joy of the LORD is your strength.—Nehemiah 8:10

- In this world you will have trouble. But take heart! I have overcome the world.—John 16:33

- A cheerful heart is good medicine, but a crushed spirit dries up the bones.—Proverbs 17:22

Here's the good news. Positive emotion can undo negative emotions. But you must choose to be intentional about it, especially if you are often around or working with negative people or experiencing especially stressful or adverse circumstances. Frederickson calls it the "broaden-and-build" theory of positive emotions. As you accumulate positive emotional experiences over time, they act as a cushion that can soften the blow when the negative events occur.

We can see how this plays out even in the simplest of events. You have a terrific day at work, a few belly laughs over the phone with a friend while driving home from work, and then someone cuts you off in traffic. You find it annoying, but you're in too good of a mood to blow up over the situation.

Now, imagine the same scenario after a terrible day at work. On the way home you get into an argument with your spouse. While you are talking, your son's school calls to tell you he got into a fight while waiting for the school bus home. Then someone rudely cuts you off in traffic. You find yourself yelling at the driver and waving your hands wildly to make sure she knows her behavior is unacceptable. What caused the difference between the two reactions? The positive emotion of a terrific day expanded your ability to deal with the minor infraction of being cut off in traffic.

Consider this same principle with much bigger life issues: persevering towards a goal in your business or career, staying focused in the face of a major health challenge, or making an important relationship work.

Negative emotions are like debits to your account. The more positive emotion you build over time, the more you are able to broaden your scope of thinking as well as your ability to handle adversity and stress.

WHEN TO MAKE DECISIONS

Negativity bias is one of the ways negative emotion can sabotage your efforts to move to the next level. In decision making, negativity bias means that your perception is literally skewed. You cannot see clearly. You go on the defensive. This is why, when you are making an important decision, you want to always make sure you are in a positive state of mind. Negative emotions such as anger, sadness, anxiety, grief, or depression will skew your perspective. Making decisions while your perspective is impaired could possibly lead to choices you later regret.

One woman I coached, Sherry, a physical therapist, was frustrated by not being promoted. When a coworker she perceived as less talented was promoted before her, Sherry quit her job before she had lined up another. Although her skills were in high demand, it took longer than she anticipated to find a job. Four months later she landed on her feet, but not before her emotional decision wreaked havoc on her finances and drained the three-month emergency fund she had so diligently saved. Have you ever made a decision in the heat of anger or frustration and later regretted it? "Let emotions subside, then decide," I once heard author Joyce Meyer say. Use this knowledge to your advantage when you need to perform.

Negative emotion narrows your scope of thinking, Dr. Frederickson explains, but you are more alert and detail-oriented after a positive emotional experience. In one study, participants were shown short videos that induced positive, negative, or neutral emotions. All the participants were then briefly shown pictures of faces. Some of the faces were of the same race as the participants while others were of a different race. Later, the participants were shown a larger number of photographs. All the original faces they'd been shown were present, along with many new faces.

Those who had experienced negative emotion prior to being shown the pictures a second time had a much more difficult time identifying the original faces of those of a different race than their own. They were experiencing what Frederickson calls "own-race bias." Those who watched something funny prior to seeing the pictures a second time were more easily able to recognize the faces of those of a different race. A burst of positive emotion actually enabled subjects to remember distinguishable features that allowed them to correctly identify subjects. Interesting, indeed.

CHRONIC UNHAPPINESS NEEDS A SURGEON GENERAL'S WARNING

An analysis of more than 30 university research studies on happiness and health by Dutch researcher Dr. Ruut Veenhoven showed that being chronically unhappy has the same effect on longevity as smoking cigarettes daily. On average, the effects of unhappiness cut your life expectancy by six years. Successful people take their happiness seriously. They don't dwell on the negative and they fill their life with the positive—positive words, positive people, and a positive outlook.

As I listened to a presentation about happiness given by Dr. Veenhoven, a noted sociologist, I was intrigued by his classification of four qualities of life that comprise overall happiness and well-being. Consider them (paraphrased below with my definitions and coaching questions) to help you determine the areas of your life in which you may have room to enhance your happiness and well-being:

1. Livability

"Livability" is about the environments in which you live, work, and play. Does your environment nurture you or drain you? Do the circumstances in which you find yourself empower you to thrive or to merely survive? What would create a more livable and happier environment for you?

2. Life abilities

Life abilities are your personal strengths, knowledge, preparation, flexibility, and potential. They can be developed, explored, and improved upon. Greater personal abilities often create more enjoyable opportunities. What talents and strengths are going underutilized in your life? What potential is going untapped?

3. Meaning

How is someone's life better because he or she crosses your path? We find the greatest meaning in life when we live the purpose for which we were divinely created. And that purpose must be good for something or someone beyond you. This element of happiness is about serving, helping, and making a difference.

4. Satisfaction

This is about your overall satisfaction with your life. Are you content with where you are? If not, what shift is it time to make? Dissatisfaction can be a catalyst for change, as long as you are honest about where you are dissatisfied. What aspects of your life bring you joy?

PRACTICAL WAYS TO BUILD POSITIVE EMOTION

One of the keys to building positive emotion is to know what brings you joy and then be disciplined about incorporating it into your everyday life. For some women—and maybe you're one of them—one of the best steps you can take is to simply lighten up! Find the joy in everyday life, even in the midst of challenges.

John 16:33 is so counterintuitive, but puts it all into perspective: "In this world you will have trouble. But take heart! I have overcome the world." In other words, trouble is to be expected. It is part of living in the world. Cheer up anyway! Don't wait for everything to be the way you want it to be to have joy. Choose joy in the midst of trouble. It is a deliberate *choice*.

The Gallup Organization, through its significant research on well-being, identified five areas of well-being—social, career, financial, physical, and community.* I would add a sixth: spiritual. In considering all six areas, you will discover many practical ways to boost your positive emotion:

Social well-being

This is about your social connections and activities. How much time do you spend in the company of others? How many close friendships do you have? Are you satisfied with the quality or quantity of time you spend with loved ones? Do you have relationships in need of repair?

---

* Tom Rath and Jim Harter, *Wellbeing* (New York: Gallup Press, 2010).

Career well-being

Choose a career that gives you daily activity you look forward to. Just as importantly, be conscious of the importance of the social component of your work. Do you feel a part of something bigger than yourself? Do you have a friend or friends at work you look forward to connecting with? In what ways do you feel a sense of contribution to the efforts of the company or organization?

Financial well-being

Look for opportunities to use your money to boost positive emotion. Give some away to people and causes near and dear to you. Use it to create positive experiences and memories you can savor for years to come. Remember the hedonic treadmill and the tendency to adapt to new "toys" when you are tempted to spend money on things you think will make you happy.

Physical well-being

Create a physical environment around you that is a sanctuary from stress. Place visual reminders around you of the things that bring you joy—for example, pictures of people and places that make you smile. Exercise frequently, and when possible, exercise with other people. Making exercise a social activity is a great way to combine two positives.

Community well-being

Beyond social well-being is community well-being. Community well-being is about the actual community you live in and the difference you make in that environment. Choose well—a safe place and surroundings must resonate with your sense of self. This aspect of well-being is also about your connection to your community. What do you do to make a difference? Research is very clear that doing good for others helps protect you from the effects of stress and negative emotion.

Spiritual well-being

Worship. Meditation. Prayer. Church attendance. All of these ways of engaging with God can dramatically impact your sense of well-being. Research even bears it out. Faith does something else as well. It gives you hope for the future, even in the face of seemingly hopeless situations. And it serves as a foundation to encourage and inspire you to engage in the five other areas on this list!

Every Woman Should Know

- Positive emotions can overcome the effects of negative emotions. By engaging in more positives, you can reverse the results of negative experiences.

- Never make an important decision when you're upset, tired, or depressed. Negative emotion narrows your scope of thinking.

- Chronic unhappiness can impact your longevity as much as smoking cigarettes every day, cutting as much as six years from your life.

PERSONAL COACHING TOOLKIT: POWER QUESTIONS TO RAISE YOUR SPIRITS

1. Who or what makes you laugh? How could you make sure to have more laughter in your life?

2. When you look back over the cumulative positive and negative experiences of your life, what do you suppose your emotional bank account looks like right now?

3. In what ways could you "lighten up"?

4. In what ways could you savor the simple but joyful moments more often? Consider time with a loved one, eating a meal, reading a good book, or having a conversation with a friend or family member.

5. What games do you like to play? Do you play often? If not, how could you incorporate more play into your life on a consistent basis?

6. What volunteer activity brings you the most positive emotion while simultaneously helping others? How could you incorporate that activity into your life consistently?

7. In whose company do you most often experience authentic positive emotion? What steps can you take to make that person a bigger part of your everyday life?

8. What is one thing you could do to create more positive emotion on a daily basis at work?

9. Are there people in your life you would get joy in bringing together? Why not move forward and be the missing link to connect others—whether through a reunion, party, lunch date, or a simple phone call?

10. Think back to a moment when you were filled with positive emotion. What happened? What aspects of that moment can you recreate in the future?

Think Differently:

Be intentional about building positive emotion in your everyday life. Be aware of the effects of negative emotion. Minimize it, and when it is unavoidable, intentionally engage in activities that boost your positive emotion in order to undo some of the effects.

Be Prepared for Battle

---✳---

*Why you must expect obstacles,
and have a proven plan to overcome them*

Key Lessons

- An optimist is constantly seeking feedback and looking for ways to improve.
- Resilience is about building an inner strength to clear the hurdles on your path.
- Don't take a leap without a Plan B.

Even looking back to my teenage years, I always wanted to lead an organization," says Sheryl Adkins-Green. "I had a vision of running a company or a division within a company." Today she is Chief Marketing Officer for Mary Kay, one of the most recognizable brands for women in the world, and responsible for all aspects of the beauty company's global product strategy and marketing efforts. "It is almost scary how consistent my role is now with what I thought I would be doing as a little girl. My love of fashion grew with my Barbie collection, and I created eye shadow with food coloring and Noxema!" she says. Sheryl's strong sense of vision has kept her focused, but it is her inner resilience that has empowered her to stay on track in the face of challenges and achieve the kind of balanced success most women hope for. She's been happily married for 22 years and has two sons she describes as "bright, confident, and creative." And she is clear about her personal mission: Creating value by connecting people and ideas.

Sheryl is a rare example of the kind of woman who is able to embody all the habits of successful *simultaneously*—she is optimistic, strategic, authentic and builds on her strengths. She cultivates strong, positive relationships, exercises self-control, and taps into her faith daily. And most importantly of all, she has consistently shown a critical key to success: Resilience.

WHAT IS RESILIENCE?

Resilience is the ability to bounce back from setbacks. Resilient people thrive and grow in the face of adversity, challenges and change. When you set out to intentionally engage in the habits of success, you can almost guarantee you will be challenged. That's life. And those who are prepared for the battles, both large and small, that inevitably ensue are the ones who will experience the most success on their path. You have to intentionally consider your options, the best preparation and the support you'll need to achieve your vision and goals.

Resilience can only be tested in the face of challenges. The woman who never accepts a challenge never know how resilient she is! You've got to go through some tough times and go *for* something to test your resilience. As you build your level of resilience, you will find yourself able to handle more and do so with more grace, peace, and effectiveness. Resilience empowers you to be effective and efficient, to navigate challenges and change, and to survive and in thrive in the face of whatever life throws your way.

WHAT EMPOWERS
YOU TO BE RESILIENT?

There are three foundational ingredients for resilience. The first you cannot change, but you can manage it by cultivating the second two ingredients.

Genetics

Genetic factors can have a huge impact on our lives. For one thing, some people are just naturally more positive than others. Positive emotion is known to strengthen you and expand your ability to handle adversity. While you can intentionally create experiences that lead to positive emotion, it does come more naturally to some. But genetics can impact your resilience in other ways as well. If a woman is genetically predisposed to a particular mental illness, for example, it is possible that symptoms of that illness may not manifest themselves until she finds herself in especially stressful circumstances. Resilience cannot be tested without a stressor.

Personal resources

Personal resources refers to your spiritual and emotional fortitude, support system, preparedness, finances, access to people, help, and opportunities—anything within your personal sphere of influence that can help you overcome challenges. You cannot succeed without strong relationships to support you. These relationships are critical for resilience. When you have a battle to fight, you don't want to be the lone soldier on the battlefield. You need others.

How you think

When faced with a stressful situation, a challenge, or adversity, what do you say to yourself? What do you think about the situation at hand? What you think predicts how you feel, what you say, and what you do. Therefore, when you intentionally *think* differently, you react differently. Let's say an unfortunate domino effect of circumstances leads to financial devastation for your family. You lose your home, your credit is ruined, and you are flat broke. As a human being, you would likely experience a range of emotions—sadness, anger, and frustration, for example. Might you also feel hopeless? Your thoughts can feed your emotions, and the thoughts that follow are particularly toxic:

- "Everything I ever worked for is gone. I don't think I could ever get it back."

- "My life and career are over. I might as well give up and accept that I'm a failure."

- "This is so embarrassing. I look like a fool to have ended up in this situation. I can't ask anyone for help because I don't want people to know the crazy situation we're in."

- "Obviously I'm not as smart as I thought I was. Otherwise I wouldn't be in this mess."

If these are the kinds of things you say to yourself, out loud or just in your head, it is only natural that you might feel hopeless. Thoughts lead to reactions—what you feel, what you say, and what you do. If you intentionally change what you say to yourself, you will change your reactions. If you find yourself thinking counterproductive thoughts like the ones above, change those thoughts to something more productive. You have that power! Try reversing that negative mindset and replacing it with words like these:

- "This is a major blow, but it's not the end of the world. I have my health. I have determination. And even though it pains me, I can start over."

- "I made some mistakes. I am going to learn from those mistakes so I don't repeat them in the future."

- "I choose to believe all things work together for good. I am determined to come out of this situation stronger and wiser."

- "I am not the only person in the world to ever go through something like this. I'm going to find a support system and inspiration from other resilient folks who have bounced back from financial setbacks."

What might you feel, say, and do if these were the thoughts you meditated on rather than the negative ones? Most likely, you would feel empowered and motivated to pick up the pieces and put your financial life back together. You would feel grateful and hopeful, rather than bitter and hopeless. You have the power to change how you feel, what you say, and what you do by intentionally changing what you think. As a man "thinks in his heart, so is he," Proverbs 23:7 (NKJV) says. Take that to heart and practice positive thinking, and you will see your resilience increase dramatically.

This simple strategy is the cornerstone of resilience. It is a secret weapon successful women use to prepare for the inevitable battles of life. It is not simply that they never have doubts or negative thoughts, but that when those thoughts show up they banish them to their proper place. They are vigilant about weeding out counterproductive thoughts and replacing them with productive ones.

Early in her career, Sheryl was offered a tough assignment that others had failed to accomplish in spite of their best efforts. As she puts it, "I was offered the opportunity to attempt a high-risk turnaround on a business that was losing money. Two previous managers had not been successful. If I was not successful, I would probably have had to move out of the company. The team was beaten down because they were failing to meet the objectives. I had to convey optimism, but also back it up with an action plan. We had to rethink and revamp every aspect of the business. And we turned it around within 18 months."

Sheryl's success in this monumental task required resilience. She was facing challenging odds. She had to inspire her team, influence management, and come up with an effective plan of action and stick with it every day for a year and a half. There were many opportunities for negative thinking to sabotage the success of the project. When resilience becomes a part of who you are and how you operate—when you make it a habit—it becomes a bit easier to maintain a resilient spirit through tough seasons, whether personally or professionally.

As you build your level of resilience by becoming more aware of your thoughts and intentionally thinking in a way that leads to productive, effective results in your life, remember this simple flow:*

Trigger ➡ Thoughts ➡ Reactions

The *trigger* is the stressor or challenge you face. It can be as simple as

---

* Karen Reivich and Andrew Shatté, *The Resilience Factor* (New York: Broadway, 2002).

a difficult conversation you need to initiate and as massive as a major life change that will take years to recover from. Your thoughts are all of the things you tell yourself about the stressor or challenge you face. If your *thoughts* were a billboard, what would they reveal? Become adept at identifying the ones that occur in the heat of the moment. Sometimes they come so quickly and automatically, they are almost subconscious. Don't allow them to be. Become aware of them so you can pull them into the light and change them. Your *reactions* are what you feel, say, and do as a result of your thoughts. Every reaction can be traced to a thought or multiple thoughts. While it may sometimes appear that we go straight from a trigger to a reaction, every reaction you have is a result of a thought. Change your thoughts and you'll change your reactions. When you choose thoughts of hope and faith, your reactions show you believe something good is going to happen. When you choose thoughts of doubt and fear, you react with anxiety, paralysis, and conversation that shows your lack of hope and faith.

WHY MUST YOU INCREASE YOUR RESILIENCE?

By our definition of resilience, you don't need it just for setbacks. You need it to live well. You need it to succeed. You need to keep disappointments, anger, and exhaustion from derailing your best plans—because they will threaten to do just that. Resilience is a way of living that empowers you not only to navigate the setbacks and unexpected turns of life and minimize obstacles on your path to success. In essence, the most resilient people can sometimes appear as though they face the fewest challenges. The truth is, they are so adept at noticing potential problems and taking action to avoid them that it appears things just come easily for them. Really, they are just doing the work on the front end.

These people have what I like to call "realistic optimism." Realistic optimists are confident about the future, but see the potential pitfalls that could very easily trip them up if they don't pay attention. Realistic optimists don't murmur and complain about problems, allowing them to become excuses for why they can't do something. Instead, they plan for them. When there is a problem, acknowledge it. Look for ways to resolve it. But be clear about what you can control and what you cannot.

In what way does this concept apply in your life right now? Is there a problem it is time to acknowledge? Is an immovable obstacle ushering you to take a detour from your path?

_____

_____

_____

_____

_____

When there is a significant risk involved in a decision, it's important to proceed with caution. This does not mean, "Don't proceed." It simply means to be wise in how you move forward. There is a fine line here though. What is risky for one person may not seem as risky for another. Risk cannot always be measured in obvious terms. Sometimes convictions and divine guidance outweigh external signs.

In 1997 I left the only full-time job I'd ever had so I could launch my own public relations firm. This move looked pretty risky to my family and friends! But I felt strongly led to do it. While I recognized there was a possibility I would fall flat on my face, I also trusted that if that happened, I could handle the fallout. That's realistic optimism at work. I believed I could succeed and I also believed failure would not mean the end of the world or the end of my career. I also recognized that I was 24 and single with no children. Failing would affect me and no one else. But even if I failed, I knew I would not regret going after my dream. I could say I'd tried. I might even regroup within a few years and try again.

The key to realistic optimism is to acknowledge the risk. What might you lose if things don't go as planned? Analyze what you will do if problems arise. Consider your plan of action and ask yourself, "Am I willing to handle that?" Whether your answer to that question is yes or no, ask yourself, "How could I reduce the amount of risk I'm taking?" Successful women have contingency plans. They rarely take a leap without a Plan B. Even if Plan B isn't fully developed, they've at least considered what the initial steps might be if Plan A doesn't pan out.

A few years after I launched my public relations firm I became clear about my life's purpose. That's when I wrote my first book. A little over a year later, I got the itch to pursue writing and speaking full-time. That "itch" came from the fact that I had finally unearthed my passion. And now that I'd gotten a taste of it, I wanted to pursue it with all my heart. But could I make it? Would I be able to earn a consistent living? What would I do if things didn't go the way I hoped? I made a decision to answer these questions. First, yes, I believed I could make it. Second, I believed I could earn a living at it. Incidentally, it took me a few years longer than I thought it would to make a decent living at it, but I was clueless when I started. That's how leaps of faith go sometimes—once you've made the jump, there's no ascending back up to the top of the cliff. You must learn to fly. And with a little resilience, you do.

But I had a Plan B as well. I answered that third question, "What would I do if things didn't go the way I hoped?" I decided I would get a job in journalism, a subject I had earned a graduate degree in but never directly pursued—and I would keep writing books. After all, having a job wouldn't preclude me from writing in the evenings or on the weekends. I already knew that, having written my first book while running another business. My Plan B didn't scare me at all. In fact, it gave me a tinge of excitement! My backup plan involved pursuing something I was qualified for but had lacked the confidence to pursue years earlier.

HOW PREPARED ARE YOU?

I want you to be able to avoid as many unnecessary obstacles and challenges as possible. That means having the foresight to think through the risks and potential challenges, then preparing well so that you are best equipped to navigate your path. That's resilience. Good preparation can mean a multitude of things. It can mean choosing the right school to prepare you for a career. It can mean choosing a profession that is aligned with your gifts, strengths, and mission in life. It can also mean observing and learning from the mistakes and successes of others before making a leap into uncharted territory, whether in business, relationships, or finances.

I quoted Sheryl Adkins-Green at the start of this chapter. When asked her mission, she's clear that it's about connecting people and ideas—something every great marketing person does. Operating in your strengths conserves your energy for the inevitable challenges that lie outside your strengths. It is difficult to be resilient when every single thing you do requires significant energy and effort.

When it comes to success, it starts with something we discussed early in this book—getting clear about your purpose or mission. How is someone's life better because they cross your path? How is your family better? How is your workplace better because you're in it? How is the world enhanced by your everyday actions? From that sense of purpose, you can create a vision that inspires and compels you to persevere, even when times are difficult. A weak vision doesn't inspire. When times are difficult, a weak vision doesn't compel you to keep going. It typically becomes a reason to quit, allowing you to pursue a vision that motivates you from within.

Success is never a straight line. We like to think it will be as we begin our journey. We get clear about our purpose. We establish a vision. We're excited about what the future holds. And then, bam! Something doesn't go the way we planned it. Have you been there? Does the unexpected throw you off course? Are you easily discouraged by a frustrating boss or backstabbing coworkers? Do you internalize failure and begin telling yourself "I am a failure" rather than "I failed this time"? Do you get drawn into negativity too easily?

The most resilient women anticipate obstacles and prepare in such a way that they are able to avoid many of the pitfalls that make the average woman stumble. The question to ask yourself is, "Am I making decisions and plans that will best prepare me for the vision I want to move towards?" When Sheryl was in high school, she chose a college based on what would best prepare her for her career. She moved halfway across the country, from Maryland to Wisconsin. "I made a conscious choice to go to school away from home. The University of Wisconsin had a strong retailing program with a strong business component. I've always been big on seeking out experiences that will prepare me for bigger challenges." She continued in preparation mode at Harvard Business School, where she earned an MBA. It was a rigorous education that would support her goals and give her a foundation that opened doors of opportunity.

But preparation doesn't have to mean a Harvard education. Preparation, as I've mentioned, means different things to different people. It is dependent upon your goals, challenges, and objectives. In many instances, it means having the patience to gain experience—and through that experience, preparing through learning. Imagine what it would be like if every child was taught how to handle money in school. By the age of 18, every child would know how to set up a household budget, save for an emergency fund, purchase a vehicle, and plan for retirement. They would know about interest rates, credit card debt, and when it is appropriate to take out a loan—whether for school, a car, or a house. If this was part of the standard curriculum in every school, do you think the next generation might have a financial advantage? It's highly likely. When people *know* better, they tend to *do* better. The same is true for you and me.

Think about a particularly challenging goal in your life. In what way could you boost your level of preparation? Consider these simple ways to be more prepared for the inevitable challenges of life:

Financial

- Save for a rainy day towards a six- to eight-month emergency fund.

- Aim to live on 80% or less of your take-home income so you have some margin for error.

- Figure out how much you need in order to retire and have a plan to get there so you can avoid a crisis later in life.

Health

- Eat plenty of fruits and vegetables so that you maximize your immune system and your ability to fight off illnesses.
- Exercise regularly to minimize the likelihood of health issues such as diabetes, stroke, and heart attack.
- Get plenty of good rest each night so that you have the energy to deal with all that you face during the day.

Relationships

- If you did not have a role model of a successful, happy marriage growing up, intentionally choose a "relationship role model" to mentor and coach you.
- Learn to love yourself before you attempt to love someone else. "Love your neighbor as yourself" doesn't amount to much if you don't love yourself.
- If you are married, talk to your spouse and set ground rules about how you will interact and communicate when you have disagreements. For example, you may agree in advance that you'll never call each other names and regardless of how angry you get, you have to kiss goodnight and sleep in the same bed.

Work

- Join a professional association or other network where you can build relationships in your field outside of your company. This way, if you are laid off or it's time to move on, you'll already have developed connections.
- Don't burn bridges, build bridges. Be friendly. See the big picture. Recognize that every battle isn't worth fighting at work. When opportunities for promotion or a raise come up, you don't want to lose out because people don't feel a connection with you.

- Be known for something. This is one of the best ways successful women navigate their way upward in a challenging work environment, being offered jobs and promotions
when others are struggling to find work. Are you the one
who gets things done quickly? Are you able to manage difficult people? Are you known for your accuracy and making sure all i's are dotted and t's crossed? Do you always
come up with creative ideas to solve company problems?
Whatever it is that sets you apart, that's your personal
brand. It's also what will keep you working and open doors
of opportunity. Resilient women know that work success is about more than just fulfilling job requirements. It's
about the added value you bring to the table. That added
value can mean added job security.

IS YOUR SUPPORT SYSTEM STRONG?

A large part of what empowers women to be resilient is a strong support system of relationships and a self-awareness that enables us to
think flexibly and strategically in the face of the inevitable challenges
that occur on the path to success. The bottom line is that women have
to be prepared for battle. We must expect obstacles. They are a normal
part of the process. We shouldn't be tripped up by them. Instead, we
must have the flexibility, optimism, and resolve to conquer the obstacles as they come—and to anticipate, prepare for, and perhaps avoid
them. Choose to have people around you who support your efforts and
can give you wise counsel.

Building a network of support starts with being intentional about
reaching, supporting others, and staying connected. Do you wait for
others to reach out to you or do you reach out to others?

I met Sheryl when she was executive at another major company and
I was brought in to assist in the promotion of a product launch. She
began reading my weekly e-newsletter and stayed in touch. She reached
out consistently via email and social media. Always genuine, generous,
and positive, her personal touch is unmistakable. And my inklings tell

me it's a big part of her success! Reaching out doesn't have to be about selling yourself or being pushy. In fact, it shouldn't be those things. It should be about being of service, being yourself, and being gracious. These are traits that are not as common as they should be, and as a result, they endear people to you. Resilient women reach out—not just when they are in need of help, but all the time. They initiate friendships and work relationships and intentionally nurture them. They build strong family relationships. They're creative about ensuring they have plenty of quality time with the people who matter most in their lives.

When describing work-life harmony, Sheryl makes a great point about the importance of being creative and realistic:

> Don't be so hard on yourself. As a working mom, you can't possibly compete with the stay-at-home mom and the woman at the office with no family commitments at home. Let go of the guilt! The time you spend with your family isn't always about the home-cooked meal, but about making time for conversation. Sometimes I'll rehearse a presentation in front of the family or let the kids help me find visuals for a presentation. Seize any and all opportunities to spend time with family, even if it's playing "Amazing Race" in the grocery store. And ask for help and accept help when it's offered.

And when describing the best decision she ever made in her life, again, it is about family. "Marrying my husband was my best decision. It blessed me with my two sons and the special qualities they inherited from their dad, and so much support along the way."

The habit of nurturing relationships and reaching out fosters resilience for a few reasons. We are strengthened by connection. We are built for relationship with others. It is in the context of relationships that we create joyful experiences, serve, and find meaning in our achievements. "Making a difference," after all, is about being a blessing to others in some way. Isolation is an ingredient for self-absorption, depression, and emptiness. It is in times of challenge, especially, that our relationships bolster our ability to overcome. By reaching out, we get advice and gain perspective. We get help. We get encouragement. We get support.

As you prepare for the battles and challenges of life, develop the habit of resilience using two ingredients you have control over: personal resources and how you think.

Every Woman Should Know

- Optimists live longer, on average, than pessimists—by as much as nine years.

- Depression has been described as the "ultimate pessimism." Women with an optimistic thinking style tend to fend off depression when bad events occur. The opposite is true for those with a pessimistic thinking style.

- In career fields such as teaching, sales, litigation, and public relations, optimism is a predictor of success.

PERSONAL COACHING TOOLKIT: POWER QUESTIONS TO ENHANCE YOUR THINKING STYLE

Answer each of these questions in a journal or with a coach or friend who can listen objectively and give you the space to explore your answers without attempting to give you the answers.

1. Spend some time in meditation. The perfect dream for you is the one God uniquely equipped you for. Paint a picture of what the next level of success looks like for you. What is your *real* dream (not the downsized one)?

2. What would it mean to you to be able to accomplish that dream? Picture yourself living that vision. What does it feel like?

3. What gifts, talents, passions, or experiences will you draw on reach your goal?

4. Think back to a time when you were at your best and reached a particularly meaningful goal. How did you do it? What did you learn about yourself?

5. Consider that meaningful goal you described in the last question. What enabled you to be at your best? Who were the people, circumstances, and other key factors surrounding your success?

6. How could you go about recreating similar circumstances to empower you to reach that "next level of success" you described in the first question?

7. Think back to a time when you failed to reach a goal. What personal factor(s) led you to fail? What external factor(s) led you to fail? What lesson(s) can you glean from these contributing factors to help you succeed when reaching future goals?

8. Realistically, when you look at the picture you painted in the first question, what are the most significant obstacles you might face? If you don't know, take a look at role models who have already been where you aim to go and pinpoint the obstacles they faced.

9. How can you reduce the risk of those obstacles occurring as you move forward? How will you navigate around those obstacles if they occur?

10. Describe your best possible future self. Who is she and how does she approach life?

Think Differently.

Be intentional about what you say to yourself when you fail as well as when you succeed. Choose hope. Dream big. Learn new skills. Believe all things are possible.

Don't Be a "Maximizer"

———※———

How overabundance can rob you of
satisfaction and make you ineffective

Key Lessons

- Embrace the idea of having enough. Don't leave behind
  good enough in pursuit of the *best*.

- Own your choices and leave behind regret.

- Be decisive and don't second-guess your decisions.

Over the years, at speaking engagements and in interviews and coaching sessions, the question pops up repeatedly. It is one of the most frequent questions I hear. Just the other day, I was asked a variation of it during a question and answer session at a women's conference in North Carolina. The interesting thing is that every person who asks this question thinks it is completely unique to them. They ask with a level of frustration and perplexity, seeming to doubt that someone might be able to provide an answer or somehow get them unstuck. Here's what it sounded like from a woman in North Carolina:

"Valorie, I have so many ideas and dreams. I love them all. I want to accomplish them all. But I cannot figure out what to pursue first. I mean, if I start in one direction, then I have to leave the other dreams behind and I don't want to do that. And I want to do the right thing, but I'm just so afraid of making the wrong choice that I am not doing anything. I am stuck. How do I choose?"

Have you ever been there? I'm not surprised at all if you answered yes. Accomplished women like you typically have multiple talents. There are many directions in which you could go. *You have options.* And that seems to be an absolute blessing—until you realize that maybe you have too many options! So many, in fact, that you cannot make up your mind! Perhaps you never thought of it this way before. Your talent and hard work have opened many doors to you. The opportunities that are so compelling have created an overabundance of choice. And rather than feeling excited that maybe you hit the jackpot, you feel buried beneath the weight of choice and paralyzed to move forward.

Soon after I finished graduate school in journalism in my early twenties, I heard a radio interview with a Grammy-winning singer. Before attaining major success in the music industry, she had worked as a secretary. The interviewer asked what she thought her secret to focus and success was. She replied, "I think my biggest blessing was that singing was all I had. I was a secretary. I didn't go to college. Singing was my talent. It was my only option. *I had to make it work.*"

Her statement was an epiphany for me. I had too many options! My talent is communication. I considered all the options for how I could use my gift—marketing, public relations, newspaper reporting, television, teaching…the list went on. There was no singular focus. I cast the net wide, and, as a result, entertained options that were never meant for me and certainly didn't fulfill me.

Can you relate? Whether you are flooded with ideas and can't determine what to pursue first or can't decide which career move to make, learning to manage your choices is one of your most critical personal skills.

FEAR AND CHOICE

Now, before I pat us all on the back for getting to a place in life where we have so many choices that we just don't know what to do, I want to point out that this predicament is often a fear-based, self-inflicted problem. Yes, of course, there are times when there are just too many ideas and opportunities and you are genuinely stumped. But there have likely been many times when the choice was obvious, but you introduced new choices out of fear.

Such was the case for me. I wanted to be a television reporter, but truth be told, I was afraid that I wouldn't be good enough. So rather than singularly pursuing what I really wanted, I dabbled in other options—ones in which I felt confident I could land an opportunity. Note: My choice was about feeling confident about what *I* could do.

Experiencing your true potential means seeing beyond what *you* can do and trusting the power of divine orchestration—the amazing opportunities that come when you are living and moving within your purpose and destiny. These types of opportunities won't be ones you create. These will be opportunities that sometimes you didn't even know existed, yet seem to land in your lap. Still, you will do the work and put forth the effort that empowers you to be ready when the opportunity shows up, and there will be no doubt that you didn't land the opportunity on your own.

Open your mind to the possibility that you may not be able to see how your vision will come together, but if you trust that it *will* come together and move towards it persistently, you will get to the next level. And the next level may be far greater than you had ever imagined. Listen to the way Paul describes God in Ephesians 3:20: "To Him who is able to do immeasurably more than all we ask or imagine, according to his power that is at work within us…" In other words, you do not even have the ability to imagine all that God can do in His infinite and abundant power.

ANALYSIS PARALYSIS

Don't be afraid to make a choice. Trust that if you start heading down the wrong path, God will correct you and gently set you on the right path. All you have to do is listen. Being tuned in spiritually is your antidote to fear when it comes to making choices and decisions. Over-analysis can lead to paralysis. Refuse to allow it in. Happily successful women are decisive. Gather the pertinent information you need to make a choice, including the information your intuition provides. Then make a choice.

"Whoever watches the wind will not plant; whoever looks at the clouds will not reap," Ecclesiastes 11:4 explains. Waiting for perfect conditions is a strategy for missed opportunities and procrastination. Disguised as prudence and caution, the process of making a choice can make it look like you are taking action and moving forward when in fact you are procrastinating. You know in your heart which is true.

The idea of having too many choices shows up in multiple ways—not just making choices about your career, but also choices in relationships, finances, your schedule, and seemingly simple matters such as what to eat or what to wear. Why is this important as you develop better thinking habits? Because happily successful women understand that while choice is good, too much choice can be bad—causing you to spend your limited time and energy in unproductive ways. Rather than making a choice and working toward accomplishing a goal in your chosen area, you're still toying with ideas that could have been dropped long ago. Rather than making quick choices about lesser priorities, you end up spending too much of your time on decisions whose consequences are not worthy of so much of your time.

Making a choice is a *thought* process. Those who are happiest and most effective think differently in terms of how they go about making choices. Equipped with the knowledge that those of us living today are bombarded with more ideas, options, and choices than any generation that has ever walked the planet, your happiness can increase dramatically just by following some intentional guidelines. I will share those guidelines in a moment, but first let's just consider the state of our culture and its impact on our thought processes on a daily basis.

WHY MORE IS LESS

Our culture of abundance has morphed into a culture of *over*abundance. More choice (abundance) is good. Gluttony of choice (overabundance) is destructive. Many women feel pressed to make the best choices and decisions about everything—and, in the process, lose sight of which decisions really matter and which decisions are a distraction. Those who strive for every choice to be perfect—whether considering a new job or which item to choose on a restaurant menu—are called "maximizers," a term coined by researcher Barry Schwartz, author of *The Paradox of Choice: How the Culture of Abundance Robs Us of Satisfaction.* Their habit of aiming for the best conceivable option in every life decision actually robs them of satisfaction and effectiveness.*

The key is to learn how to stop being a maximizer and start being a "satisficer," according to Dr. Schwartz. The term "satisficer" is a combination of *satisfy* and *suffice.* It is about setting the minimum standard you'll need in order to be satisfied and deciding that when you find the situation or answer that meets that minimum, it will suffice. You are free to move on to other choices that need to be made. You let go of the anxiety that plagues maximizers—the fear that something better might be out there. It doesn't matter. You found an answer that will suffice and your time and energy can be better spent moving on to other matters.

To be clear, satisficers are not slackers by any stretch. They are more content and more efficient in their work. They miss fewer important opportunities because they have the time to focus on the things that truly matter. Maximizers are more likely to get stuck, spend their resources trying to keep up with the Jones, and be depressed. As America has become a wealthier nation with more choices than ever, rates of happiness have decreased and depression has increased tenfold. You can learn to make choices and decisions that increase success and happiness, and ultimately create greater mental and spiritual well-being. Here's the basic premise of Schwartz's work:

- Voluntarily limit your choices rather than evaluating every available option. We are a nation that celebrates freedom of choice, but too much choice can limit you more than it frees you. The key is to understand your priorities and needs and clarify the ultimate goal of any given choice. In other words,

---

* Barry Schwartz, *The Paradox of Choice* (New York: Harper Perennial, 2004).

some choices are far weightier than others and deserve more time and attention, while others deserve very little.

- Determine what is "good enough" in most instances, rather than insisting every choice be about finding the absolute best option. Note that I did not advise you to have minimal standards. Quite the contrary: your standards may be quite high. And your standards, for any given decision, may be quite different from anyone else's. Finding what's good enough is about getting in touch with your authentic priorities and desires. It is an internal decision—a gut check—rather than an external one based on impressing or gaining the approval of others. Set criteria that meets your minimum standards.

- Lower your expectations about the outcome of any given decision. Most of us have come to see the phrase "lower your expectations" as purely negative. But hear me out on this. We often believe that our choices will make us happier than they actually will. Remember the hedonic treadmill we discussed in an earlier chapter? Much of the reason you fret over a given choice or decision is because of the impact you believe that choice will ultimately have on your happiness. You believe that new job will solve your lack of happiness. And maybe it will make you happier for a time, but after you get the job, you may discover that your lack of happiness is a deeper issue. Maybe it's the spirit of discontentment you need to address, not a career transition. If you lower your expectation about what you believe a decision will give you, you can often see more clearly and even remove some of the intensity and anxiety over the decision.

- Make your decisions irreversible. This is another counterintuitive strategy, but research shows it works. When you make your decision irreversible, you are less likely to second-guess yourself or look for ways out. Instead, you stick with it and find ways to be content with it.

- Stop comparing your decision with everyone else's!

REGRET

Have you ever made a decision only to later daydream about what it might have been like had you made a different choice? Do you fret even when you make a good choice because you later discover there might have been an even better alternative? When you evaluate your success, do you think about the opportunities you passed up along the way?

"If only" thinking decreases your satisfaction with the choices you make, even when those choices are good ones. Maximizers are far more likely to experience regret—and sometimes they experience it before they even make a decision. The mere thought that they might make the wrong decision leads them to anticipate regret, and the accompanying feelings of anxiety and disappointment soon follow.

When opportunity costs are high, regret is more likely. An opportunity cost is what you give up in order to move forward with a particular decision. A woman I worked with named Bria had recently landed a cushy position with a large entertainment public relations agency in New York. Because of her stellar media contacts in the industry, winning Bria over was a major coup for her boss. They rolled out the red carpet for her. She was humbled by it, but also appreciative. She felt a sense of gratitude and loyalty not only towards her boss, but the others at the company who made the offer so good for her. They gave her the best accounts to work on and generous bonuses, but just a year into her tenure on the team, a major motion picture studio called from Los Angeles. They wanted Bria to come on board to head publicity and strategy for the entire company.

It was the job she'd dreamed of since college—a dream 25 years in the making. She and her husband had both grown up in southern California, and always wanted to get back to the West Coast. The offer was tremendous—higher salary, greater autonomy, flexible working arrangements, and lots of sunshine.

But Bria was torn and losing sleep over the decision. She felt obligated to stay at the firm that had been so loyal and generous. She was worried about her reputation in the industry and damaging relationships with people who had worked so hard to win her over and keep her happy. She was faced with major opportunity costs. If she didn't take the job offer in Los Angeles, when would she get the chance to move to California again—with a relocation package? How could she say no to her dream job? If she took the offer in Los Angeles, there were no guarantees she'd like the company. Should she give up a great job at a great company with great coworkers and move her family across the entire country for the unknown?

When opportunity costs are high, it is these types of questions that can get you stuck while you are trying to make a decision, thereby delaying the process. But after you make your decision, these questions can still persist as you begin to second-guess your choice. Have you been there? It is impossible to be happily successful when you are in the shaky territory of wondering whether you are where you should be. Second-guessing creates an inner environment of discontentment. This discontentment disturbs your peace and undermines happiness.

A successful woman's thought processes create fulfillment. An important element of fulfillment is contentment. Happily successful women manage their thoughts around their decisions in such a way as to minimize regret. What decisions are you regretting right now? Consider your relationships, career, finances, health, and spiritual life, and note those decisions here:

_____

_____

_____

_____

_____

Why is it so important to minimize regret? First, regret is not all bad. Regret is sometimes appropriate. If you make a poor decision, it would be denial to pretend it was a good decision. You should be concerned if you cannot recognize when you make a poor decision, because this denial indicates that you may be in danger of repeating that decision in the future. However, there is a difference between regretting a decision, learning from it, forgiving yourself, and moving on…and regretting a decision, beating yourself up about it, and then regretting it some more.

Perpetual regret is unproductive thinking. If you are to move your life to the next level, there is truly no room for it. It often leads to rumination—habitually rethinking negative thoughts about past experiences. Rumination can lead to pessimism, which will impact your ability to clearly see your possibilities for the future.

Pessimism can also lead to depression, a state which can debilitate you and your ability to take steps in the right direction. Regret can also prevent you from making future decisions. It creates a sense of fear that you will make even worse and more regrettable decisions. Think differently by noticing your propensity to second-guess or regret your decisions, large and small. Here's how to minimize or eliminate regret:

Embrace the habit of satisficing

Satisficers have a key habit that enables them to minimize regret. They make a decision about the minimum standards that will satisfy them for any given decision. At work, satisficing can be a key to productivity and progress. Rather than insisting on perfection for every single task and project, be clear about which projects you can truly afford to spend more time "perfecting," and which ones will be fine to set lower minimum standards for. For example, satisficing about an internal report that is still in draft status may mean just getting a few ideas on paper so that you can start the brainstorming process in a meeting. Satisficing about the final presentation based on those ideas to be presented to the client will mean a higher standard and more time, but the payoff will be worth it.

If you are buying a sofa, for example, you could set a minimum standard—under $800, deep cushions for sleeping, soft and comfortable, between 70 and 80 inches in length to fit the space, and dark in color so that it will wear well. Once you find a sofa that meets all of those criteria, you can stop looking! Sure, there may be a cheaper or softer sofa somewhere, but you don't have to keep searching for it. You found one that will work.

Spend time before a decision clarifying what you want. Then give yourself permission to make a choice once you find the option that satisfies these minimum standards you set. When you satifice, you acknowledge that there may be better options out there. But your goal is not finding the best. Your goal is finding the most convenient option that meets your minimum standards.

You won't be upset if something else comes along that is a little better because you realize that there will be a cost for landing that option. It will require more of your resources, whether time, money, or emotional energy. And you are preserving your resources for other more important matters. You are not obsessed with the perfection. You are aiming for progress and contentment.

Don't look at too many options

The more options you consider, the more opportunity there is for the sort of comparisons that leads to regret. Narrow your choices. By satificing, you will already have created criteria that should allow you to cut some choices from consideration. Be vigilant about limiting your choices so that you do not become overwhelmed, which can lead to paralysis. Be focused. Be intentional. Don't waste your time on options that really aren't options.

Focus on the good in your choices, not the bad

The more you focus on the negative aspect of a choice, the more likely you are to regret it. Once you've made your choice, choose to focus on the positive. Gratitude fosters contentment. Contentment with your choices is what you are after.

OWN YOUR DECISIONS

Another important element of eliminating regret is to own your choices. It can be tempting to make choices and then behave as though your choices were not choices at all. Instead, you tell yourself, you had no other option. But the truth is that you always have more options. Sometimes those options are not ones you would like very much, but they are options nonetheless.

For example, perhaps you don't like your current job, but you choose to get up every day and go to it. That's a choice. What is the alternative? Well, there's always the radical choice to quit. I'm not suggesting you quit without a game plan or another position already lined up, but you *could*. Acknowledging that fact can free you to realize that you have made a choice to stay put right now. Own that decision. Then make a plan to put yourself in position to do something you love for a living. Making that plan is a new choice.

Owning your decisions is about embracing your life as it currently stands and embracing your power to make new decisions. These decisions can change the course of your life. It is very empowering to own your decisions, whether good or bad ones. When you own your good decisions, you build confidence in your ability to make more of them.

Women who have made many good decisions over their lifetime often do not give themselves credit for where they are in life. But happily successful women don't play that game of false humility. They look back over their lives and acknowledge the major decision points that have led them to where they stand today.

Can you do that? Let's stop for a moment and celebrate your good choices. Answer this question on the blanks below: What are the five best decisions you have ever made in your life? Consider all five of the key areas—relationships, work, finances, physical health, and spiritual life:

Relationships

_____

_____

_____

Work

Finances

Health

Spiritual Life

_____

_____

_____

_____

_____

What is the most important lesson you gleaned from each of those choices?

Relationships

_____

_____

_____

_____

_____

Work

_____

_____

_____

_____

Finances

_____

Health

Spiritual Life

By noticing your good decisions and choices, you acknowledge your decision-making ability. This builds self-efficacy, your belief that you can do what you set out to do. By identifying the lessons, you reinforce them as you move ahead to make new decisions and choices in critical areas of your life based on previous lessons.

By the same token, happily successful women don't just look back over their lives at the major decision points worthy of celebration. They acknowledge the major decisions they'd make differently if they had known then what they know now. This, too, takes confidence. It is the confidence that emerges when you truly own your decisions and choices—all of your decisions and choices, even the bad ones.

This level of self-awareness reveals an authenticity that fosters resilience and acceptance of yourself, warts and all. Noticing bad decisions can even help you see patterns you may want to break. You can make a conscious choice to break those patterns, but only if you notice them. Noticing them requires this type of self-reflection.

My client Kate worked through this exercise and learned a powerful lesson for her life. At the age of 36, she reflected on decisions she'd made since college that had caused her to change course several times. She chose a major, but during her senior year she changed her mind about going into that field. Rather than spending an extra year pursuing a degree better suited to her now that she was clear about her desired career path, she decided to stick with her original major.

She graduated, but without the background she needed. So she went back to school to study what she really wanted to do. But upon graduation with a second degree, she took a job that was not in the field she studied.

Sounds ridiculous, right? Why go to school for something and then not pursue it? Kate never asked herself that question. After several years on the job, she became frustrated for not having pursued her dream. So once again, she changed course. Still, she didn't directly pursue her real dream. Because she is a hard worker and intelligent, though, she was promoted several times, eventually becoming a director in her company.

Her personal life seemed to be another series of chaotic choices. Kate was not intentional about pursuing the kind of relationships that would lead to what she really wanted—marriage and a family. Almost haphazardly, Kate seemed to end up in relationships with men who couldn't commit. Even when she knew they had trouble with commitment, she persevered in the relationships, hoping they'd change.

By the time Kate came to me for coaching, she was frustrated and exhausted by some of the results she was getting in her life. Smart and accomplished in so many ways, Kate felt unfulfilled. From the outside, most people would describe her as successful. But that description was purely based on external achievements. She was good at her work, but didn't enjoy it very much. She was thoughtful and giving in her relationships, but rarely felt that others were as thoughtful and giving towards her. Worst of all, she could not see how her choices contributed to her challenges.

In Kate's mind, she was a victim of others' behavior and choices rather than a conscious participant who made choices every day—choices that led to her frustrations. Through coaching, Kate began to see that the choices she had made all along the way formed a pattern. In our first coaching session, I pointed out three choices she'd made that contributed to her current circumstances:

- She chose to earn a second degree, but not pursue a career in it against her heart's desire.

- She chose to change careers, but not in the direction of her authentic dream.

- Over the course of eight years, she chose to remain in three successive relationships with men who had no intention of marrying her.

"Have you owned any of these decisions, Kate?" I asked.

"What do you mean *owned* them?" she asked.

"Do you see that these were choices you made? You could have chosen a different path, but you chose these actions instead," I explained gently.

"I never thought of it that way," she admitted. "I guess I kind of felt like I didn't really have a choice. I didn't have the contacts to get a job in the field I wanted, so I went in a different direction."

"Would it have been possible for you to consciously build contacts in the field you wanted?" I probed. Kate thought for a few seconds.

"Well, that might have taken some time, but I suppose if I had started doing that ten years ago, then yes, within a few years, I might have been able to break into the field," she said reflectively, with a tinge of optimism in her voice.

"How about the ex-boyfriends? How about the current one? Did they all let you know they were not going to commit, or did they say they wanted to get married and then changed their minds?" I asked.

Kate got quiet, then laughed lightly but sarcastically. "Well, one of them didn't come out and say it, but he just kept pushing off the subject. The second boyfriend as well as my current one have had some really bad relationships. My current one was hurt badly by his ex-wife and he's just scared to take the plunge again," she explained.

"So these last two men carried baggage from their old relationships into a relationship with you, and this explains why they couldn't commit to you?" I asked.

"Yes," Kate said emphatically.

"Have you ever been hurt badly in a relationship, Kate?" I asked.

"Yes, in all three of these relationships, actually," she said.

"And yet you still want to open yourself to marriage?"

"Yes, I think marriage is a good thing," Kate said. "I don't think I can't have real love in the future just because I've been hurt in the past."

"So why do you make excuses for men who don't share your attitude towards being hurt? You are choosing to commit to someone who refuses to commit to you. That's a choice," I told her.

Over time, Kate began to see that by not setting standards and being conscious about her choices, she had made decisions that were contrary to her true desires. Previously, she had not seen these as choices, but rather as circumstances beyond her control. By building her self-awareness, she could now own the series of choices that led her to her place of frustration.

By intentionally noticing your poor choices and decisions, you can see patterns in your behavior that may be sabotaging your success. To go to the next level, it is essential that you notice your poor decisions and glean lessons from them so you do not continue to repeat them. Just as you identified the best choices you've made in your life, I invite you now to notice the worst choices and decisions you've made. List here the five worst decisions or choices you've made:

Relationships

_____
_____
_____
_____
_____
_____

Work

_____
_____
_____
_____
_____

Finances

_____
_____
_____
_____
_____

Health

_____
_____

_____

_____

_____

_____

Spiritual Life

_____

_____

_____

_____

_____

What is the most important lesson you gleaned from each of those choices?

Relationships

_____

_____

_____

_____

_____

Work

_____

_____

_____

_____

_____

_____

Finances

_____

_____

_____

_____

_____

Health

_____

_____

_____

_____

_____

Spiritual Life

_____

_____

_____

_____

Start owning your choices and you'll be empowered to truly own your life. Your eyes will be opened to the ways in which you have the power to impact your own future. You will become more comfortable in your own skin. You will be less likely to feel sorry for yourself because you will finally see that you are not a victim of circumstance, but rather a person who can choose how to respond to circumstances that come her way.

When you are clear about your values, standards, and needs, the opportunity to make a conscious choice in any given circumstance becomes clear. When you are making a career choice, your values and needs can help you see that an opportunity that looks good on the surface may not be right for you. When making a decision in a relationship, you can evaluate your choices and make wise decisions about how to proceed. If a situation doesn't meet the criteria, you know better how to categorize it. The bottom line is this: You don't have to entertain every option that comes your way. You make choices daily. Make them consciously. Own your decisions.

BE DECISIVE

Being decisive doesn't necessarily mean being hasty. You may deliberate over your decision for a while, but once you make it, you stick with it. Making a choice to stick with your decisions once you've made them can help alleviate regret by shifting your focus from how you could have made a different choice (in the past) to how you can make the most of your choice (in the present). This kind of decisiveness frees your energy to focus forward rather than staring backward at what could have been, or even what could be if you go back and try to undo what is already done.

This process is about raising your awareness of the thoughts that come to you and the ones you choose to entertain. Making a choice that your decisions are final is a strategy that conserves energy and creates stability rather than second-guessing. Trust me: the grass is rarely greener on the other side. Be decisive. Take the time you need to make an informed decision. Then, once you make your decision, stick with it. The most successful women are often those who are willing to persevere through challenges and disappointments until they make it to the other side.

REIGN IN YOUR PERFECTIONISM

Do you keep putting off goals because the timing just isn't right? Is it difficult to complete any project because you're still putting the finishing touches on it? Do your family and coworkers accuse you of being impossible to please?

You know where this is going. You're a perfectionist. In a coy sort of way, you might even be proud of it. You call it being "thoughtful," "conscientious," "excellent at what you do." You may be all of those things, but sometimes you are also "anxious," "stressed," and "perpetually dissatisfied."

Perfectionists are more likely to put off making a decision. They procrastinate. And they are less happy than those who have high standards, but who aren't obsessed with perfection. If you aren't careful, perfectionism can cause you to miss the joy in the journey as you focus exclusively on the destination. If this sounds like you, try these three strategies to reign in your perfectionism habit:

1. Focus on progress, not perfection.

Get a clear sense of the purpose in everything you do. Then it will be easier to know which things deserve that extra time to get things just right, and which things don't.

2. Set your minimum standard and stop when you meet it.

Today, we are bombarded with more choices and options than ever before. It can be easy to get stuck in a cycle of trying to make every choice the perfect choice, but research shows that people who do this are more anxious and less content. Whether you are deciding what to order off the menu or which new television to buy, get clear about your minimum standards—and once you find an answer that meets those minimum standards, choose it. Stop searching for more options. Save yourself the stress and start satisficing.

3. If you must perfect something, perfect your top priority.

If you are a hard core perfectionist, get clear about your top priority. Give yourself permission to perfect that, but refuse to spend valuable extra time trying to perfect the things that do not top your priority list. After all, if you're going to get just one thing right, make sure it's the thing that has the most impact.

AUTOMATE THE FREQUENT CHOICES

In order to focus on what really matters, it is sometimes necessary to free up time by creating shortcuts on activities that are not a priority. If you are like many women, you spend a great deal of time and energy each day making a series of minor choices. Whether you're deciding which outfit to wear, what to have for lunch, or what to cook for dinner, some decisions should be placed on autopilot.

Take a moment to identify all the choices you make on a daily or weekly basis that you could make a blanket decision about now. For example, could you create a weekly or monthly menu and repeat it indefinitely? Or lay out two weeks' worth of outfits for work, then repeat it every two weeks. When the seasons change, identify a new ten-day rotation. Make a decision once and repeat that choice for a specified period of time. Automate your frequent choices and free up your energy to focus on what really matters.

PERSONAL COACHING TOOLKIT: SATISFICE YOUR LIFE

1. In what ways are you a maximizer? Give a specific example

of how this tendency has shown up recently and wasted time or resources.

2. What is the most important decision in front of you right now? Why is the decision so important?

3. What minimum standards and criteria can you set for making the right choice in this decision? In other words, how could you satisfice?

4. What choices do you most often second-guess?

5. What could you do differently to end your second-guessing over this choice?

6. What frequent, little choices could you automate?

7. Look back at your list of your five best decisions and the lessons you learned from them. How could you apply these lessons to a current situation?

8. Look back at your list of your five worst decisions and the lessons you learned from them. How could you apply your most important lessons to the important decision you need to make right now?

9. In what way do you allow discontentment to steal your joy? What could you do to be more content?

10. What decision do you sense God nudging you toward right now? Is it time to move forward with that decision?

Think Differently:

Recognize that having choices is good for your well-being, but too many choices can be overwhelming. Be intentional about clarifying your standards and needs so you can "satisfice" more and "maximize" less.

Don't Go It Alone

---※---

*Why authentic connections are more important
than ever and how you can cultivate them*

Key Lessons:

- Strong relationships increase your resilience
- Daily social interaction is essential for your well-being
- Successful women collaborate, communicate, and celebrate each other

---

At a speaking engagement several years ago I was speaking with a fellow author I admire, and felt it was time to reveal my little procrastination secret. Since she's written more than 20 books and sold several million copies, I thought she could give me some advice on how to become more disciplined and finally kick my procrastination habit for good. I also thought she'd be shocked by my admission. Surely an award-winning writer of 20 years couldn't relate to such inconsistent writing habits.

"I really want to get better at writing consistently and not procrastinating," I said.

"Tell me about it," she said. "Last summer, I procrastinated so long working on a book that I ended up having to miss my own family vacation! Everybody else left and I stayed home because I was already so far behind on my deadline, the publisher finally put their foot down."

I was stunned. "Do you always procrastinate?" I asked.

"A lot," she admitted. "But that was my worst case of it."

I'd thought I was the only one. Isn't that often the case? We think our problem is so different from everyone else's. And when you think that, you give the problem more power than it deserves. You make it unique. You beat yourself up about it. And worst of all, you don't open your eyes to the solutions and support that exist. You can't make a change until you stop hiding your challenge and begin sharing it.

A habit that will accelerate your success and increase your happiness more than anything else is reaching out, making authentic connections, and celebrating with others.

LEARN FROM OTHERS

It starts with making authentic connections. Every truly successful woman makes them. It will accelerate your goals and shorten your learning curve. Be honest about where you are and actively seek to learn from the experiences of other like-minded people. No need to reinvent the wheel! And there is certainly no need to believe that your challenge is new. In fact, as King Solomon proclaimed in Ecclesiastes 1:9, "there is nothing new under the sun."

Indeed, there isn't. There is no need to hide your challenges as though they are something to be ashamed of. When you are willing to connect authentically—to admit when you are struggling or unsure of how to handle a situation—you will often find your answers through connection with other people.

I challenge you to acknowledge an area you'd like to strengthen and then ask yourself these coaching questions:

Coach You: Accountability Questions

- Who do I know that has conquered this habit?
- What lessons or wisdom can I glean from them?
- Who do I know that is *ready* to conquer this habit?

- Do they want to be accountability partners as we reach towards the goal?
- What specific milestones will mark our progress as we move toward the goal?

Don't beat yourself up for your bad habit. Instead, find common ground with those who can relate—and make a connection that pulls you in the right direction.

BUILDING A COALITION

When Colleen Rouse and her husband, Dennis, moved to Atlanta in 1990, their network consisted of two couples they'd met in Bible college in Tulsa, Oklahoma, three students they'd known at the University of Georgia, and a handful of friends from Dennis's high school days in a town 30 miles south of the city. But they were equipped with a vision and the boldness to believe that they could meet enough people to make the vision come to fruition. That vision was a big one.

They planted themselves in a suburb on the north side of Atlanta and believed in their calling to racial reconciliation. "We wrote it down," Pastor Colleen explains. "We saw thousands in our vision. And it had been prophesied to us that there would be multiple thousands."

But that vision didn't look too promising in the beginning. "One weekend, we took the whole church out to dinner," she recalls. "It was one couple and us." They thanked the couple for their faithfulness and renewed their commitment to the vision, not looking at the circumstances, but instead trusting that things would come together. The following weekend, 33 visitors came to their service. They grew by about 100 members per year those first few years, but the congregation was largely homogenous and Caucasian.

Soon senior co-pastor Dennis Rouse began asking members to invite others to visit the church—others who didn't look like them. The members did just what he asked. Slowly but surely, the church grew more diverse. Today, Victory World Church lives up to its name and vision. With more than 10,000 members representing 105 nations, it is one of the most racially diverse churches in America, if not *the* most diverse.

"We constantly cast vision," says Pastor Colleen, who is senior co-pastor along with her husband. "Our leadership style is very relational and servant-based. The people on our staff are not here to serve my dream. I'm here to help them realize theirs."

From the beginning, Pastor Colleen and her husband understood they would not be able to accomplish their vision alone. Not only did the two of them agree on the vision and pursue it together, but they actively and enthusiastically shared the vision with others who believed in it and served alongside them to bring it to pass. There is power in connection.

In what ways do you need to connect more deeply in your relationships and community? Are you attempting to go it alone? Are you focused more on the goal than the process? Do you resist opportunities to collaborate with others? "My definition of success centers around people more than it does achieving any particular task," says Pastor Colleen. "It has everything to do with the legacy that I leave behind in relationships and the people I am able to cheer on."

FULFILLMENT HAPPENS
THROUGH CONNECTION

Success rarely happens in isolation. When it does, it is less gratifying. Our sense of meaning and purpose is fulfilled in relationship to our impact on others. The most successful women are those who have built positive relationships that form a personal and enduring community of family, friends, colleagues, and neighbors.

In surveys of more than two million employees, the Gallup Organization found that the most reliable predictor of productivity at work was whether an employee answered yes to the question, "Do you have a best friend at work?" As the pace of life has become busier, jobs are more mobile and Americans live farther away from family and friends.

The prospect of building a sense of personal and professional community is much more challenging. Ecclesiastes 4:9-12 perhaps sums it up best:

> Two are better than one,
>   because they have a good return for their labor:
> If either of them falls down,
>   one can help the other up.
> But pity anyone who falls
>   and has no one to help them up.
> Also, if two lie down together, they will keep warm.
>   But how can one keep warm alone?
> Though one may be overpowered,
>   two can defend themselves.
> A cord of three strands is not quickly broken.

We live in a culture that values individualism. It is an attitude that permeates the workplace, entertainment, sports, and even the family structure. One of the most common reasons adults cite for not wanting to start a family is that children "infringe on personal freedom." More people live alone and work alone than ever before. Much of this change is due to the freedom technology allows, but that freedom can also lead to isolation and self-centeredness—and neither is an ingredient in the recipe for success.

FIVE QUESTIONS TO ASK A MENTOR

One of the most common questions I get from those looking to advance their career or business is, "How do I find a mentor?" We're all looking for someone who's been there, done that to walk with us along our path, steady us when we stumble, and offer a wise voice of experience in times of uncertainty. But often when a person of experience and substance is standing right in front of them, people don't know the right questions to ask. A person you deem a role model or mentor often won't have a program laid out for you to follow, but many are willing to answer questions and share lessons from their own life experiences if you will just know what to ask when the opportunity presents itself.

Mentorship is often an informal relationship, so you learn to glean information in a casual, confident way by asking insightful questions that can shorten your learning curve on the way to your goals. Here are a few questions to ask when you have the opportunity to converse with someone whose experience could prove invaluable to you. Intuitively choose which questions to ask and when. Then create a few questions of your own. If your mentor of choice were sitting with you right now, what would you want to know?

1. What is the best decision you ever made?

Often, at a pivotal moment, successful people make decisions that might go under the radar as the "best" decision. Once you ask, you'll see how good decisions can impact the course of your life for years to come.

2. What's the worst decision you ever made?

Listen carefully to this answer so you can avoid making the same mistake. Ask why it was the worst decision and what they would do differently if they had known better.

3. If there was one thing you wish you'd known when you started, what would it be?

Talk about a question that can shorten your learning curve quickly. Hindsight is always 20/20, right? Make your mentor's hindsight your foresight.

4. When you face a setback or disappointment, what do you do?

Successful people are often those who can see the good even when things go badly. Those who succeed are usually those most willing to take risks, and risk takers are comfortable with failure as a part of the journey to success. A Japanese proverb says, "Fall seven times. Stand up eight." Find out what your mentor does from a mental and emotional standpoint to keep getting back up.

5. What is the wisest step you think I could take in my career right now?

Given your current strengths and weaknesses, threats and opportunities, what is the best piece of advice this mentor could offer you right now? After you've gleaned lessons from their life, you might already guess what advice they'd give you. But to be certain, ask. Be open to constructive criticism and feedback. Don't fight it. Embrace it.

INCREASE YOUR INFLUENCE ON THE JOB

Ever feel like your ideas aren't being heard at work? You can turn things around by shifting your approach. If you do, you'll also shift opportunities your way—promotions, better assignments, and maybe even a higher salary. In a recent appearance on CNN, I shared with viewers these six strategies to wield more influence. I hope you'll find them useful too.

1. See the big picture

Influence is not just about knowing what you want. Even more important is knowing what others want. If you know what others want and focus on helping them get it, they are far more likely to help you reach your goals. Understand your company's goals—not just your department's goals. See the big picture and where you fit into it.

2. Rise above the fray

With an awareness of the big picture, you're less likely to get pulled into negativity and coworker drama that won't pay off. Set yourself apart by choosing your battles wisely. Why waste energy on situations that diminish your influence? You'll only make enemies and make yourself look petty. Always ask, "Will this situation matter a month or year from now?" If the answer is no, let it go.

3. Stay focused on solutions

Many people focus on problems. You want to focus on solutions. Every problem presents an opportunity for you to demonstrate your problem-solving skills—and every company needs problem solvers! When problems arise, don't go to your boss about it until you've answered the question, "What are three potential solutions?" Then when you approach your boss, you're coming as someone who makes her job easier (and influences her decisions in the process).

4. Tap into unofficial networks

Every organization has unofficial circles of influence—they eat lunch together, smoke together, take breaks together, and talk around the water cooler. Influence isn't just about who has the big title, but who people listen to. Tune in and notice who the influencers are. Build trust and reciprocal relationships with them. Be interested in what matters to them.

5. Start small

First, make it easy for your boss to say yes by finding small things you want to influence. Getting a decision maker to say yes once makes it easier for them to say yes again. Build trust by starting small. Then expand your influence from there.

6. Plan what you say

Influencers are strategic. When it's time to ask for something, spend some time—even if just a minute or two—planning how to ask. When is a good time? What groundwork do you need to lay? Do you need to get a few others on board first? What is the best way to phrase what you have to say so the other person will feel positive about saying yes?

Every Woman Should Know

- People who have a best friend at work are seven times more likely to be engaged in their work, produce higher-quality work, and have higher overall sense of well-being.

- Research shows you need about six hours of social time daily. Reach out, make that call, eat together, and be social!

PERSONAL COACHING TOOLKIT: POWER QUESTIONS TO BUILD AND MAINTAIN AUTHENTIC RELATIONSHIPS

1. In what way is it time to stop going it alone?

2. In what ways can you let go of your isolation? Paint a vivid picture that empowers you to tap into the power of connection.

3. Who are your three closest confidants?

4. Among your closest confidants, what specific step could you take to strengthen each of those relationships?

5. When it comes to relationships, whether personal or professional, what do you fear most? What would you do differently if you let go of that fear? Why is that important to you?

6. Who are your mentors in each of the following areas? If you don't have a mentor in any one of these areas, who can be your role model? What connections can you develop in your search for a mentor?

   Relationships

   Health

   Work

   Finances

   Spiritual life

7. Take a look back at the five questions to ask a mentor or someone who has "been there, done that." Who will you ask these questions? When?

8. A key element of success is service. Who are you a role model for? What impact do you most want to have on that person?

9. How much social time do you get each day? In what way could you improve the quality (and if needed, quantity) of that social time?

10. In what ways do you want to have more influence at work? What specifically would you like to influence over the next month? The next year?

Think Differently:

Make it your success strategy to not go it alone. Choose your relationships intentionally and nurture them consistently.

Write It Down

---- ✳ ----

*The revealing reasons you need to tap into
the power of the pen starting today*

Write down the revelation and make it plain on tablets, so
that a herald may run with it. For the revelation awaits an
appointed time; it speaks of the end and will not prove
false.—Habakkuk 2:2-3

Harriette Cole was a seventh grader when a few "mean girls"
turned her otherwise happy, preteen life into a middle school
nightmare. What Harriette did with that experience took her
on a journey that made her stronger and more authentic. Here is how
she described her childhood experience to me:

> When I was growing up, my best friend from kindergarten
> until seventh grade became mad at me about something. I
> don't even remember exactly what. So she convinced my
> group of friends to not be friends with me anymore. She
> literally convinced *all* my friends not to speak to me. I real-
> ized it when my teacher posted on the board that I got 100
> percent on a test. I was mortified by that, not wanting all
> the attention it brought. I rushed out to speak to my friends
> and they simply would not speak to me. I spoke louder, but
> they ignored me. They jointly decided to act as though I
> wasn't there. And for a very long time, this continued.
>
> I went home devastated and my mom convinced me to tell
> her what happened. She said, "They are not your friends."

As hard as it was, I decided she was right. My heart was broken. I loved my friends and now all of them were suddenly not my friends. I made a decision though, to survive. I made a bunch of changes. I got new glasses, cut my long hair to just one inch long, changed my class schedule—and I decided to model and write.

I began to write about what I was going through. Journaling, for me, was like breathing. At first it sounded more like whining, but eventually my journals weren't just about my difficulties, but also my dreams. Through journaling, in particular, I became a good writer. I could hide in my books. I focused on school more. I decided the people who were my friends were my sisters, my family. I became a writer, a good writer, based on a negative experience.

For Harriette, writing became a lifeline—and a pathway to success. It helped her be resilient through a painful, unexpected experience. "Most people who are driven to success have had some kind of major painful thing happen at some point in their lives," she says. "But in spite of the pain, they have the resilience to push forward."

Today, Harriette Cole has accomplished pretty much every goal she has set for herself: Host a national television show. *Check.* Author a nationally syndicated newspaper column. *Check.* Become editor at a major national magazine. *Check* (well, four checks actually). Write a national bestseller. *Check.* Conduct workshops across the country to help people learn to be more of who they already are. *Check.*

From Mary J. Blige to Alicia Keyes, Harriette Cole has taught artists and executives how to simple *be.* She served as Creative Director and Editor-in-Chief of *Ebony* magazine, and runs Harriette Cole Media. "The biggest problem for many women is not that they don't dream big," she warns. "It's that they don't dream at all." It is that dead zone of buried dreams that threatens the happiness, and ultimately the success, of millions of women.

It was through a painful childhood experience that Harriette discovered her true self. And through it, she launched a successful career and life as an entrepreneur, wife, and, joyously, a mom.

Dr. Laura King, a researcher at Southern Methodist University, has confirmed that writing through traumatic life experiences is a powerful strategy for getting through difficult times and even learning from them. Interestingly, writers did not have to come to any resolution or take any specific action to benefit from writing about their painful experiences. It seems that simply writing about what happened and taking the time to describe it was enough to yield positive emotional results.

Writing is a tool for processing events, and this act of processing proves to be therapeutic. In some ways, writing simply validates your experience. It acknowledges it. If you write from a truthful place, whatever that truth is, you have the opportunity to benefit tremendously from the conscious art of writing. After writing earnestly and from the heart, writing can sometimes give you a third person experience. Putting experiences on the page, and especially re-reading those experiences, makes you a witness to your own life.

That in itself is a very powerful experience. You don't often get to experience yourself outside of yourself, and when you do, you often are able to see yourself more objectively. Have you ever seen yourself in a photo and thought, "I didn't know that outfit looked like that"? Or watched yourself on video and gained a whole new perspective? Looking at you can be quite a different experience than *being* you.

YOUR BEST POSSIBLE FUTURE SELF

Dr. King's research has also found that writing about life goals is beneficial. It actually has health benefits and gives the writer a stronger immune system to ward off infections. One of the exercises she prescribes that leads to positive emotion and health benefits is to write about your best possible future self. You simply write about your life in the future, using present tense. Imagine what your best possible self is like at some given point in the future. How does she feel? Who is she with? What does her day look like? Where is she? Who does she impact? What is different about your best possible future self compared to your current self? Write as vividly and specifically as you can about your best possible self. Envision yourself there.

TURNING POINTS
AND *AHA!* MOMENTS

Get into the habit of putting your thoughts on paper. Harriette's journaling not only empowered her to bounce back as a young girl abandoned by her friends, but it was a turning point toward the fulfillment of her destiny. Her journaling led her directly to her passion and purpose in life. Fashion and writing has shaped her career. The modeling she began as a teenager continued in college at Howard University in Washington, DC. Her passion for style eventually led her to *Essence* magazine, where she became a fashion editor. And her career took off from there. But the common thread through it all is that she has never stopped writing.

How about you? I know I've asked you lots of questions throughout this book and invited you to write through your answers. Have you done it? Be honest. If you haven't, I encourage you to go back and start writing! There is reason Habbakuk advises, "Write down the revelation and make it plain" (2:2). There is a thoroughness to your thought process that occurs through writing that doesn't occur when you simply sit and think about your challenges and goals. By writing, you get things out of your head. As you do, you make room for more thoughts to come. And these thoughts often provide the clarity you need. This process simply cannot happen when you only think things through, but never write things through. Successful women know the power of the written word.

The other advantage of writing your thoughts rather than simply thinking them is that you keep a record. It is so easy to have an *aha!* moment—we get little ones all the time when we're disciplined about prayer and meditation—and then lose it. Don't lose the aha moments. Capture them on paper. This will empower you to track your progress, recapture great ideas, and remind yourself later of wisdom you had long ago. I am amazed when I look back at my journals at how many of my dreams have come to pass. And it is also interesting to begin making sense of the negative patterns and habits that have been around too long. It can give you the fuel to make decisions about the challenge you need to conquer next.

WHAT IF I DON'T WRITE WELL?

My first rule of writing, even when I'm starting to write a book, is this: Be willing to write badly! Just get started. Get something on paper. It's kind of like turning on a faucet that hasn't been used in a while. When you first turn it on, the water may spurt and bubble or look a little rusty. But if you let it flow a little while, eventually the water will become clear. Your writing is the same way. Let it come out rusty. If you allow it to keep flowing, the good stuff will make its way to the surface. And besides, the pages you write when you journal are for your eyes only. Make a decision not to judge yourself harshly.

The words you write become insight. They become coaching. They become therapy. They become healing. They become excitement. They become gratitude. They become possibility. They become vision.

HOW OFTEN SHOULD I WRITE?

I don't much appreciate the word "should" and I avoid it as much as possible. I will not tell you how often you should write, but I will tell you this: Write often. Daily if you can. But if not, don't pressure yourself and certainly don't beat yourself up for writing less. If you only get to do it once a week, that's fine. Just do it consistently. You don't have to write a novel. You might just write a paragraph or two some days, while at other times you write three or four pages. It depends on what's on your mind. Just get in the habit. The more you do it, the more it comes a part of your lifestyle. As a success strategy, it will be worth it.

SLOW AND STEADY

Here is something else writing does for you. It forces you to slow down. It causes you to pause and take notice of your life. Remember our chapter on resilience? Taking your thoughts captive begins with being self-aware. Self-awareness is impossible when you are on autopilot. When you constantly go-go-go and never slow down to catch your breath, you will rarely notice your thoughts, the impact of your actions, and the opportunities in front of you. An adjustment to your approach will change your life and work for the better.

Writing at a specific time and on specific days can become a personal method you use to develop self-control, slow down, and be more intentional about your life. If you know you'll be writing every morning before you start your day or every evening before you go to bed, you have a scheduled appointment for personal growth. You have a sacred place to notice what's right in your life and a place to explore solutions for what's wrong. Success is intentional, and writing is a powerful way to be intentional.

THREE BLESSINGS

Another piece of research that confirms the power of writing is called the Three Blessings exercise. Researchers have studied individuals who write down three blessings before going to bed at night. Those who do so consistently for three weeks have experienced deeper sleep, fewer colds, and less anxiety than those who don't. Interestingly, the study didn't yield the same results when subjects only counted their blessings in their head or verbally. The key is to write them down. Again, there is power in the written word.

SELF-COACHING THROUGH WRITING

As a personal and executive coach, one of the most meaningful goals I set for myself is to teach my clients to coach themselves. The answers you need to experience your potential and navigate the challenges and opportunities you face lie within you, not me. My job is simply to be a catalyst, a vessel to ask you the right questions so that you can access the divine answers that already exist for you. But it is absolutely beautiful when you can begin to ask yourself the right questions on your own, and answer them. My ultimate goal is to help you coach yourself to the next level of success. I can't change your life, but you certainly can. And writing is a powerful tool to do so.

Throughout these pages, you've seen me write coaching dialogue. I pose a question and show you how it was answered in real time. I did that to model for you what it looks like to self-coach. It is not hard. It simply takes intention and honesty. Ask the questions that are inklings. Ask the obvious. Then answer. Then ask the next most obvious question. Ask the question you've been avoiding. And when you get stuck, ask yourself, "If I knew the answer, what would it be?" "If the Lord Himself were sitting here, what would He tell you to do?" These are simple yet profound questions. Get into the habit of asking and then answering your own questions. Here is a list of 31 starter questions (one for each day of your first month of self-coaching) to get you started on your journaling quest. I encourage you to come up with a list of your own questions that intrigue you:

1. What's the best thing that happened today? Why is that so great?

2. What's really holding me back? (Go beyond the surface answers of *time, money,* and *family* to get to the real answer.)

3. What am I afraid of?

4. What am I afraid will happen? (The difference between these two questions is only slight, but it may yield a different answer entirely.)

5. How do I want someone's life to be better when they cross my path?

6. What if I fail at this? What then?

7. What if I am not good enough? What will I do then?

8. What if I don't know enough? What then?

9. What if my worst fear comes true? How would I handle that?

10. Who do I most want to impact and how?

11. What is my top priority in life right now?

12. What is my vision for my life?

13. What am I avoiding?

14. When am I at my best? (Write lots of details to help you create your winning success formula!)

15. When am I at my worst? (Write lots of details to help you get vigilant about eliminating these conditions.)

16. What's my bucket list? (All the things you want to do before you "kick the bucket.")

17. Which thing on my bucket list do I want to do next? What's the first step to making that happen and when will I take that step?

18. How do I want to feel with my spouse/child/coworker? (Follow up: What would enable that feeling?)

19. How would my life change if I…?

20. What have I always wished to accomplish?

21. What conversation is it time to have?

22. What's my gut reaction?

23. What do I really want?

24. What opportunity does this challenge present?

25. What message is being offered in this situation?

26. What do I want to be different in my life one year from now?

27. What goal would really get me excited?

28. What goal is most important to me right now? What would it feel like to stretch that goal?

29. What are the small but meaningful milestones I can set to keep myself motivated on the journey to my goal?

30. How do I want to celebrate my next milestone?

31. What or who is draining my energy right now?

WRITING FOR A BREAKTHROUGH

Writing gives you clarity, and there is perhaps no time you need clarity more than in the face of fear. As you pursue bigger dreams, inspired by a purposeful vision, it is inevitable that you will face fear. As we've discussed on these pages already, fear is normal for everyone at every level of success. The difference between women who succeed at the high levels and those who do not is their ability to muster courage and keep fear from dictating their actions—or the lack thereof. One of the most important questions you can answer in the face of fear is, "What if?"

Never allow a "What if?" question to linger and intimidate you without facing it head-on and answering it. It may feel scary, but that's to be expected. When you face it head-on, you take away its power to paralyze you.

Take that mental journey to the place you fear most. It's the place where "what if?" leads. When you don't answer a "what if?" question, its power multiplies because the assumption (in our minds, anyway) is that the answer to the question is something you could not handle. But is that really true? I mean, what could happen if you moved toward a goal or took action to address a challenge that you literally could not handle? And what is the definition of "could not handle" anyway?

Typically, "could not handle," when you really peel back the layers beneath your fear, means you would be embarrassed. Perhaps you would lose something of importance to you or become depressed or overwhelmed by the situation. But peel one layer beneath that outcome, and you'll really get somewhere. So let's say you were embarrassed, what would you do then? Embarrassment won't lead to death. So what exactly would you do if you were terribly embarrassed? I'll tell you what you'd do. After you cried and rehashed it in your mind and maybe even talked about it with your best friend or went to a therapist because you just "couldn't handle it" anymore, you'd move on with your life. You'd adjust. You'd move on. Being the happily successful woman you are, you'd eventually learn from it. You'd glean the lesson and maybe even try again. Bolstered by the realization that the world did not come to an end, you'd be stronger for it. And you'd have no regrets, because you actually took action in the face of fear and survived!

When you write through your "what if?" questions, you give yourself the opportunity to time travel into a fear-induced future and get a glimpse of what would happen. This process will at times be uncomfortable. You may tremble as you write. You may shed a tear. You may even feel like you are being silly or fatalistic. Don't let any of that stop you. This exercise is one of the most powerful ways to use writing to muster the courage to walk into a more successful future. I call it writing for a breakthrough.

If you are not in tune with your what-if questions, here are a few of the most common ones for women:

- What if I fail?
- What if I don't have enough experience?
- What if s/he/they disapprove?
- What if I am rejected?
- What if my idea gets stolen?
- What if I succeed and they expect me to keep performing at a higher level and I can't handle it?
- What if I'm not as good as I think I am?
- What if I end up old and alone?
- What if my children don't turn out well because of my mothering mistakes?
- What if I don't have enough money to retire?
- What if I lose my job?

The self-coaching process you can use to answer these questions is to peel back layers by asking a follow-up question. It's not enough to answer the "what if?" question and stop. Answer it, then ask the following questions until you get to an answer that allows your mind to feel complete. Paint a picture of what the future might look like should this "what if?" come true. Here are some follow up questions that will assist you as you write:

- What's the worst part of that?
- What scares you most about that?

- If that happened, what does that mean to you?
- What would you do then?

Writing is a tool. It is a tool for self-coaching. It is a tool for exploration. It is a tool for self-awareness that builds resilience. It is a tool for goal setting. It is a tool for self-control. And if used consistently for your personal growth and success, it will improve your health and well-being. As you keep going to new levels, use your writing as a constant companion to help you get there.

Every Woman Should Know

- Writing a goal down on paper dramatically increases the likelihood you will achieve it.
- Licensed therapists often use writing as a tool to help patients heal and reduce anxiety about the future.
- Writing about your life goals is good for your health and has been proven to strengthen your immune system.

PERSONAL COACHING TOOLKIT: POWER QUESTIONS TO HELP YOU WRITE THE ANSWER

1. What are your hesitations about making writing a consistent part of your successful lifestyle?

2. When is the best time of day for you to write consistently?

3. Is there any pain that you've yet to heal from or forgive? Will you try writing about it? Remember, you don't even have to find a solution for it. Just writing about what happened and how you felt can help you process the experience and begin to move forward.

4. Consider the key areas of your life: health, work, relationship, finances, and spiritual life. In what area do you most

need a breakthrough? What would a breakthrough in this area look like?

5. When will you begin writing for a breakthrough in that area?

6. What is the biggest challenge you face today? Will you try writing through it and see what you discover?

7. What is the biggest opportunity you have right now? What do you want to see happen with this opportunity? Write about it.

8. Think of the goal that is nearest and dearest to your heart. What will the accomplishment of that goal symbolize for you? How will it feel to achieve it?

9. In what way do you most often get stuck when attempting to move to a higher level of success?

10. How can you ensure you stay on track with your writing life-style? In other words, what specific reminders or things can you put in place to make it easy to do?

Think Differently:

Adopt writing as a success tool that empowers you to reflect, self-coach, and strategize through the challenges and opportunities of life.

Conclusion

———✳———

I t has been a joy to walk with you through the pages of this book, exploring habits that make you happier, healthier, and more resilient. Remember, behaviors become habits when we practice them over time and make them a part of our lifestyle. I hope you'll revisit these pages and use this book as a reference whenever you need a boost or a simple reminder of what you already know!

At the end of a coaching session, I always ask my clients to share with me the most valuable insight they want to remember from the session. It helps them mentally pinpoint the most meaningful nugget. So I'm curious, what's been most helpful for you from *Successful Women Think Differently*? What's the most meaningful action you'll take as a result of reading the book? I'd love to hear your answer! You can share it with me at www.facebook.com/valorieburtonfanpage. I read every message and can't wait to hear from you. And if you want more inspiration from week to week, just visit me at www.valorieburton.com to subscribe to my free weekly e-newsletter, "The Coaching Session." I look forward to continuing to encourage you with practical steps that help you experience your potential.

As you move into the next season of your life, I wish you great happiness, health, and resilience.

Until our paths cross again ...

Warm wishes,

Valorie

Coaching Guide

———— ✳ ————

The strategies and ideas on these pages make for great group discussion. You've figured out by now that as a coach, I believe wholeheartedly in the power of asking the right questions. When you ask the right questions, you get the right answers. Being able to talk out those answers in a welcoming setting can be powerful, sparking *aha!* moments and authentic communication. Below are some powerful coaching and discussion questions related to topics in the book. These questions can guide you towards clarity and the next steps to become happier, healthier, and more resilient. Use them in your small group, with friends or family.

STRENGTHS VS. WEAKNESSES

Think Differently: Remember that it is far more effective to build on your strengths than to fix weaknesses.

1. What weakness(es) do you tend to focus on? What do you think would happen if you finally accepted your weaknesses and found a way to use your strengths to work around them?

2. In your opinion, what is your greatest strength? What do others point out as one of your top strengths? Do you agree with them? If not, is it time to *start* agreeing with them?

3. Consider your biggest goal or challenge right now. How could you use one of your strengths to succeed?

MAXIMIZING VS. SATISFICING

Think Differently: With so much on your plate and so many choices and options, it is essential to your happiness, effectiveness, and well-being to set standards you are comfortable with and make choices that meet your standards—and stop searching for the ever-elusive better option. Otherwise, you will waste time and energy with a never-satisfied pursuit of perfection.

1. What is the most common way you maximize? How has it impacted you and your ability to find satisfaction in reaching your goals?

2. Consider your answer to question #1. If you were to "satisfice" in that area, what would it look like?

3. What are you afraid you will miss out on if you stop maximizing?

CULTIVATING POSITIVE EMOTION

Think Differently: Positive emotion has multiple good effects on your mind and body. It can help you live longer, be healthier, and manage adversity and stress. In relationships, try to keep a ratio of 3:1 of positive to negative interaction to facilitate effective communication and bonds.

1. What do you think of the 3:1 positive to negative emotion ratio (5:1 in marriages)? In what relationship(s) do you need to increase that ratio?

2. Chronic unhappiness can have the same impact as smoking cigarettes daily in terms of how it impacts your longevity. What does that say to you about the importance of taking your happiness seriously and taking action to be happier?

3. What is causing you unnecessary negative emotion? What will you do to release that from your life and work?

SEEING THE GOOD
(MOST OF THE TIME)

Think Differently: Optimists make better leaders, succeed at higher levels, and live longer. They also explain their failures and successes differently, which is a trait those who are more pessimistic can develop in order to be more effective in life and work.

1. When do you tend to be pessimistic? Has your pessimism helped or hurt you, and how?

2. Who in your life can help you be a "realistic optimist"? (If you're a pessimist, it's someone who is more optimistic. If you're an optimist, it's someone who is a bit more pessimistic.)

3. Research shows optimists explain successes as personal (I did it!), pervasive (it affects everything I do!), and permanent (it happened this time; it can happen again!). Do you struggle with taking credit for your successes because you see your successes as a blessing from God? What is the right balance between acknowledging your own effort and talent and acknowledging favor and blessings?

GETTING OFF THE
HEDONIC TREADMILL

Think Differently: We are not the best predictors of what will bring lasting happiness, which means you can find yourself in a never-ending pursuit of things and accomplishments—to no avail. When on the hedonic treadmill, once you achieve or acquire something new, you adapt to it and need something bigger and better.

1. In what way(s) have you ever found yourself on the hedonic treadmill? Is it possible you're on it now?

2. Happiness is 40 percent intentional activities. What are some of the key activities in your "happiness action plan"?

3. Have you ever noticed certain triggers that deplete your happiness or draw you to a less joyful place (i.e., stress, certain events, etc.)?

BUILDING SELF-CONTROL

Think Differently: Studies show self-control and consistent practice are better predictors of success than talent.

1. In what area of your life do you want to build more self-control?

2. What is one consistent action you could take to improve upon your greatest talent?

3. If you took this action daily, how would your level of success differ from where it stands now? Be specific.

WRITING YOUR WAY TO SUCCESS

Think Differently: Writing about life goals and challenges has a positive effect on your health, ability to process emotions, and reach goals.

1. How do you describe your "best possible future self"? Did you do this exercise in the chapter "Write It Down"?

2. Have you given yourself permission to write badly? Doing so can help alleviate the anxiety that keeps some women from using writing as a success tool.

3. In this age of texts, e-mail, and computer-based writing, is it harder for you to put pen to paper than it used to be? What is the easiest way for you to write?

MAKING AUTHENTIC CONNECTIONS

Think Differently: Strong relationships are a cornerstone of happiness and authentic success. Learn to connect authentically with people and success will follow.

1. How is technology or work overload impacting your most important relationships?

2. In what way(s) do you need to practice more authenticity in your life? Do you ever struggle to just be yourself? When?

3. For the most important goal you want to reach right now, who is your role model? Who is your mentor? If you are missing either, in what way could you reach out?

Coaching is a powerful process that helps you get clarity and take steps towards the life you are meant to live. To learn more about coaching, personal development and coach training programs, visit www.capp institute.com.

Valorie Burton is a certified personal and executive coach who has served hundreds of clients in over 40 states and seven countries. She is founder and director of The Coaching and Positive Psychology (CaPP) Institute and the author of six books on personal development. She is deeply committed to helping people be more resilient so they can thrive in life and work, be more productive, and live with balance and purpose.

To learn more about The CaPP Institute's coach training and corporate training programs, visit www.cappinstitute.com

To learn more about books by Valorie Burton or
to read sample chapters, log on to our website:

www.harvesthousepublishers.com

HARVEST HOUSE PUBLISHERS
EUGENE, OREGON